BACK OF BEYOND

Memories of Life on a Holderness Farm
1903-1925

by
Alice M Markham

Edited by
John Markham

Sketches by
Trevor Galvin

Highgate of Beverley
Highgate Publications (Beverley) Limited
2010

British Library Cataloguing in Publication Data.
A catalogue record for this book is available from the British Library.

First published by Lockington Publishing Company Ltd., 1979 (ISBN 0-905490-09-6)

ISBN 978-1-902645-54-4

Highgate of Beverley

Highgate Publications (Beverley) Limited
24 Wylies Road, Beverley, HU17 7AP. Telephone (01482) 866826

Produced by Highgate Print Limited
24 Wylies Road, Beverley, HU17 7AP. Telephone (01482) 866826

Contents

PREFACE

Back of Beyond was published in 1979 by Lockington Publishing Company, a pioneering publisher in the days when new local books were far less frequent than they are today. In the last 30 years publishing has been transformed both nationally and locally and for some time I have toyed with the idea of bringing out a new edition in a revised format under the Highgate imprint.

An ideal opportunity has come with the extensive restoration of St Andrew's church, Paull, and ambitious plans of a number of enthusiasts to make the church more accessible to visitors and to encourage more to enjoy the village and its story by producing a heritage trail. As Paull features so prominently in *Back of Beyond* this seemed the perfect time to issue a new edition, with all profits going to the church.

As I explained in the 1979 preface, the book originated in a series of lectures I was giving for the (now gone and much lamented) Hull University's Department of Adult Education, entitled 'The Edwardian Age in East Yorkshire'. One advantage of studying this period was that there were still plenty of people around who knew it at first hand or were familiar with the reminiscences of their own relations. I grew up listening to my mother's stories of a childhood on a remote Holderness farm in the early years of the 20th century and these proved to be interesting talking points on which to hang a discussion.

Some years before, she had made a brief attempt to write down some of her memories but·there had been no progress for a long time. I suggested she start again. Beginning to write the opening chapter of a new book on a blank piece of paper is a daunting prospect and I eased the way by giving her the same list of topics I had used in the class – the family, food, school and so on – to focus thoughts and revive memories: a useful method for those considering something similar. When I read what she had written I asked questions, which resulted in more writing. The book was not written as a consecutive narrative but was put together in its final form as a joint venture.

The text appears, with a few minor amendments, as it was in the first edition – with the exception of names which were previously omitted. My mother was reluctant to break confidences and to make public disclosure of the private lives of people, some of whom had been dead for many years. But another 30 years have since passed and Sue Hyde, who has worked with me on this edition, suggested it would be helpful to readers if a family tree were included and the names of the principal characters in the story inserted in the text. A few relevant footnotes have been added.

Another suggestion Sue made I have readily adopted. The 1979 edition began with an introduction in which I placed the memoirs in a wider regional and national context. Life at the farm was lived far from the madding crowd and the people there were distanced from events and developments which were making the news. My aim in the introduction was to fill in some of these gaps. Only in the case of the school had I access to any original material or undertaken anything which could, even remotely, be described as 'research'.

Sue realised, however, that the most important part of the book was the memoir and preceding it by a fairly lengthy introduction created an obstacle to be overcome before one arrived at a vivid and sometimes moving personal story. Accordingly I have now converted this historical material into a section, 'Background to *Back of Beyond*', which I have placed, more logically, after the reminiscences.

My mother died in 1990 in her 87th year, outliving all her brothers and sisters, most by many years. Comments and letters from readers brought her great pleasure and getting out of her system the horrors of school, which remained a trauma even into old age, must have been a therapeutic process. At least I hope so.

John Markham

Acknowledgements

I am extremely grateful to Sue Hyde, who produced a new text from the original version of this book and has made many valuable suggestions for improvement. Tony Leake, the present tenant of Little Humber Farm, has been most helpful in many ways and gave an informative guided tour of the farm to myself and artist Trevor Galvin, whose sketches have considerably enhanced this new edition. I acknowledge with thanks the work of Sheila Gardner, who has researched the Norfolk background of the Gardner family. Paul Cross ws extremely helpful by providing information from the 1911 Census and on Miss Jenkins, 'Rabbit Nanny'.

As always, I express my indebtedness to Barry Sage and Barry Ireland for their professional services.

Back of Beyond
1903-1925

by
Alice M Markham

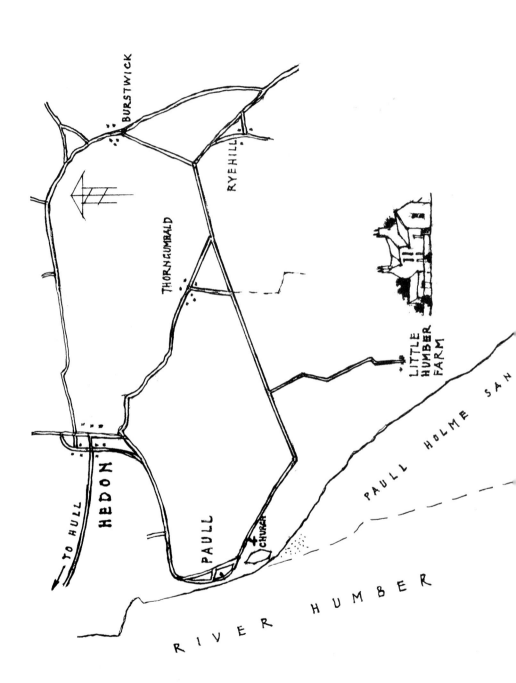

BURSTWICK

RYEHILL

THORNGUMBALD

LITTLE HUMBER FARM

PAULL HOLME SAN

TO HULL

HEDON

PAULL

CHURCH

RIVER HUMBER

HOME AND FAMILY

I was born in 1903 at Little Humber Farm in the parish of Paull in East Yorkshire where my father, John Henry Gardner, was manager – usually known as the foreman – for William Richardson, who rented his farm from the Constables. They lived in a very big house called Burton Constable Hall and owned a lot of land in the area. It was a very lonely farm, three miles from any village and approached by rather a winding road which passed only a few odd farms.

We were near the Humber in an unsheltered, bleak, flat area with few trees, and we felt the strong easterly winds which seemed to be blowing much of the time. Most of the fields ran up to the bank which had been built to protect the land from the river, but sometimes high tides came over in places where rabbits had made holes. There were very many rabbits which did a lot of damage to the crops, and the farm men used to raise a bit of extra money by snaring them and selling them at half-a-crown each.

Although it could be bleak and lonely, as children we had many happy times on the banks of the river, and it is an area for which I have great feeling. One of the nicest sounds I remember was going to the Humber after the tide had been up and hearing the river banks all settling again, little pools of water running here and there and the seabirds calling out as they found anything and everything the tide had left behind. The smell was one I never forget – fresh salty air and a beautiful smell from tufts of small flowers whose name I think was Thrift. I feel I can still hear the gurgling of the water finding its way over the mud flats.

Our house was quite a new one and I think my father and mother were the first to live in it. It was also the first house they had ever had. Until my parents[1] married, my mother lived with her uncle and aunt at Welwick, a small village 14 miles away, and she remained there after her marriage while her husband worked in another village; it was there, too, that their first child, Annie Elizabeth, was born. My mother often told us about her upbringing at Welwick. Her uncle and aunt were very religious people. Sunday was very strictly observed and everyone went to church, her uncle wearing a high top hat. No sewing, knitting or games were allowed.

My mother was a very clever needlewoman, and crocheting was one of her main

---

1   John Henry Gardner and Maria Jane Robinson were married at St Luke's church, Hull, in 1890, perhaps surprisingly as they were such country people. Both gave Hull addresses. The explanation appears to be that their first child, Annie Elizabeth, was born on 26 July, only a few weeks after her parents' wedding on 14 June. The birth took place in her mother's home village, Welwick; no doubt the marriage date of the new Mrs Gardner would not be widely known. The bridegroom is recorded on the marriage certificate simply as 'Henry' (he was generally known as 'Harry' and his bride as 'Jane' ('Jinnie'). He was 21 and her age is given as 19, though she was, in fact, 17. Her father's name is recorded as John Robinson, although her birth certificate states only her mother's name, Hannah Robinson, and the father's name is omitted. Whether there was such a man or whether this was a way of concealing the truth is not known.

interests. I remember her telling us how she once walked to Patrington to look in a shop window displaying crochet mats so she cold go back home and copy the pattern she had studied and remembered. She loved doing that kind of work, but my father always said it was a waste of time.

It was a big undertaking for my father to work at Little Humber as foreman,[2] as he was only in his early twenties and the farm was between three and four hundred acres in size. Obviously the farmer, William Richardson, realised that he was very able and had confidence in him. The land was very hard to work, but it produced very good wheat. My father was very strict with the men and as a result he was not liked. The farmer, however, had told him that he did not want him to work himself but to see that the men worked, and gave him a free hand with everything on the farm. My father made it quite clear that everybody had to do as he said. I have known him get men out of bed at night when he discovered that they had neglected the horses in some small way. I always felt very sorry for them. The farm men addressed him as 'Foreman' or 'Master', which they pronounced as 'Maister'.

My mother and father had been married very young and always seemed young to us. My mother had black hair and a most lovely complexion. Her skin was like silk to touch. She was very kind and just lived for her family. Although she had very little time for pleasure she always looked neat and tidy even while working. The dresses she wore when working in the home were grey and black striped, with white collars. She was always busy; she made all my father's shirts and knitted long woollen stockings for him. I would describe my mother as very Victorian. She would not allow us to sew or play games on Sundays and we were sent to Sunday School as soon as we were old enough.

My father, on the other hand, was a very strict man and we were all afraid of his harsh words. Sometimes he seemed so nice, but there was always a feeling of fear which never left me until long after I was grown up. We had to clean his best boots and the leggings

which he sometimes wore. They all looked like glass, they were so bright. He was a very vain man and liked admiring himself in the looking-glass. My mother had to starch his collars and these had to perfect. He wore them, however, only at the week-end when he went to Thorngumbald and there was a sigh of relief when he had gone out, for he made such a fuss. Everyone had to reach 'this' or 'that'. There was a great performance when he had a shave. He used a cut-throat

The author's father

---

2 Early references to him in parish registers and on certificates describe him as 'farm labourer', supporting the view that he was talent-spotted by the farmer and given his promotion.

4

The author, circa 1917

razor which he sharpened very expertly on a leather strop, and he sat at the kitchen table with a mirror in front of him. I rarely heard my father address my mother by her Christian name, Jinnie. He would often just shout, 'Are you there?' I often felt sorry and unhappy for my mother but she always said she was pleased that she had us children and we all felt free with her alone. We dare sing and have a jolly time when my father was out but a sudden quietness descended as soon as he entered the house.

I was the fifth child in a family of eight, two boys and six girls.[3] My mother had all her eight babies born at home and worked hard right up to the time of the birth. One of my aunts would then come for a short period and help until she was strong enough to get up. I expect she was working again with a very short time!

I was told that my eldest sister, Annie, was at home when I was born (which was just before Christmas) and that she cooked a leg of mutton for Christmas dinner and took it upstairs to my mother to see if it was properly cooked.

Our house[4] was five-bedroomed and had a large kitchen, a back kitchen, and a front room. There was also a dairy down three steps which sometimes flooded but was a wonderfully cool place for keeping food fresh. The kitchen, the most important room in the house, had two wide wooden tables, one of them very large, and long wooden seats. The large table was used by the farm men, the smaller one by our family. There was a large cooking range with a boiler at the side which held two bucketsful of water. A coal fire heated the oven and a constant supply of wood was needed to get the oven hot enough for cooking. A wagon would also be sent over to Hedon Station for a load of coal.

As our family was so large and there were always men living in who had to be provided with all their meals – and who had very big appetites – it was a never-ending struggle for my mother to provide enough food for the meals which everybody ate in the kitchen. Of course, the girls in the family all had to help as soon as they were old enough and we became experienced cooks at a very young age. At the end of the kitchen stood a large flour bin which could hold 40 stone of flour but which needed to be continually refilled by the miller who made regular visits to our house. There was a regular routine of housework which was rarely changed. Monday, of course, was washday, followed by ironing on Tuesday. Wednesday was a baking day, and the bedrooms were 'done' on Thursdays. Friday was another day for a big baking session before the weekend, although no day went by without hours spent on baking.

Washday meant a lot of really hard work with very simple implements – a wash tub, a dolly tub and a dolly stick, and an old-fashioned mangle with wooden rollers. We used no soap powder, just bars of white kitchen soap and washing soda. When the clothes lines were full we spread the washing on the hedge.

Oil lamps (either hanging or standing on a table) were used for lighting and we also had kelly lamps and candles for the bedrooms. We had a pump for water for washing and cooking, but all our drinking water had to be fetched by watercart (a large barrel on

---

3   As already noted (see note 1 above), the first child, Annie Elizabeth, was born in Welwick. For some undiscovered reason the third child (and first boy), George Henry, was born in Thorngumbald, though by then (1895) his parents were living at Little Humber and had had another daughter, Ada, born there in 1892. His birth may have been at the home of his paternal grandparents, James and Hannah Gardner.

4   The house was demolished in the mid-1970s. It was built of Paull bricks of such poor quality that they could not be salvaged.

The stackyard. The now demolished foreman's house, where the author lived, stood to its rear

wheels) from a spring pump two miles away near the watch-tower, Paull Holme.[5] The water from our own pump had a very funny taste, and was not suitable for drinking. If we wanted a bath we had to take a tin bath upstairs and then carry up buckets of hot water from the copper. The water was used by more than one person. In spite of this we always had a weekly bath.

There were no taps in the house, just a bowl on a stand, and after my sister, Agnes,[6] two years younger than myself, died of diphtheria, all the drains and sinks had to be moved further away from the house. I have a very early memory of her. I can plainly remember her taking all her clothes off except for her little shirt outside in the paddock near our house. I was four when she died. Even when I turned five I did not start school and no one seemed to bother us. I suppose it was because we were three miles from the school and it was considered too far for me to walk at that age.

The small front room which led off the kitchen was very cosy. It contained a couch, chairs, a table and a sideboard, and the floor was mostly covered with pricked rugs. On the walls there were two cases of stuffed birds, a duck, an owl and a stoat, and a wall clock with a carved horse at the top hung at the end of the room. In the winter we would often have a fire in the front room for the evening, but my father preferred to stay in the kitchen. He would borrow a copy of the *Yorkshire Post* which the farmer had delivered by post. When he had finished reading it he would sit sleeping and snoring. In fact, he always had a sleep in his chair before going to bed. We only bought a weekly newspaper ourselves, the *Hull News*, but my grandmother Gardner who lived in Thorngumbald, took the *News of the World* and sent it along for my parents. We were given strict instructions that we were not to look at it, and when she gave it to us to take home I seem to remember she tied it up with string. Of course, this only made us more curious and we loved to have a peep inside.

My own bedroom, which was at the front of the house and looked out over the stackyard, was small and just contained a bed, a wash-stand, a jug and bowl and a chest of drawers. My mother's bedroom, however, always seemed so nice. It had a bed with a carved foot, and a canopy with curtains at the head, and I thought it great fun to get into her bed and draw the curtains round me. It was the only room upstairs with a fireplace in it and what a treat it was in winter to have a fire and to be allowed to get undressed in front of it before going to our beds. I remember my eldest sister, Annie, telling the rest of us fairy stories as we sat around the fire.

There were always farm men living in the house who slept in double beds in a room at the back known as the 'Men's Chamber'. As there was a separate entrance to it we could lock our back door and they could still get into their bedroom by a ladder which led through a trap door. This ladder was scrubbed white each week, and the men were not allowed to go up it wearing boots. The sweat from their stockinged feet did, however, stain the whiteness of the wood. The men's room was scrubbed out every two weeks and the floor, like the ladder, was as white as driven snow. No carpets were allowed. It was a never-ending job coping with all the work in the house and I still wake up sometimes, afraid that I have forgotten to make the men's beds!

Across the windows were iron bars. I never really knew why, though I was told it was to stop them running away because they were engaged for a year at a time. They were

---

5   The only surviving part of a medieval manor house.

6   Agnes, born 1905, died 1907.

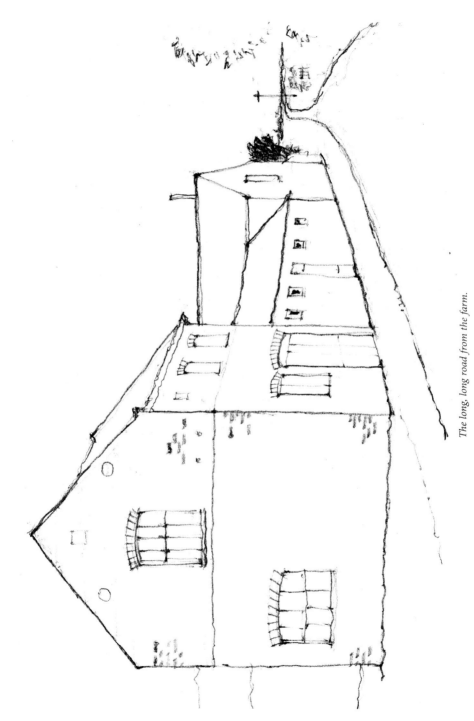

The long, long road from the farm.

allowed their boxes with their clothes in and, although a chamber pot was provided, it was not to be used unless absolutely necessary.

Before their breakfast at 6 o'clock they had to do an hour's work outside, attending to the horses and so on. My father would knock on the wall of their chamber to wake them up and each man had a lantern which he had to use in the early winter mornings as it was still dark. These lamps had to be cleaned and filled with paraffin so that they were always ready when wanted. At 6 o'clock my father called them in with a shout of 'Breakfast time!' and took the head of the men's table as he did every breakfast except on Sunday when he ate at the family table. He also took his dinner with the men, but had his tea with the family.

In the evenings when work was finished they would sit around the saddle room. In winter they were allowed a fire and they passed the time away at such things as cards and playing the mouth organ. The saddle room was really like an old cottage room. It had a brick floor, a fireplace, a table fastened to the window, a stool or two and a form. The saddles were hung on the wall at one end. The fire used to burn really well in there and heat up the whole place. At one time one of the men who was a bit of a wanderer and had no home slept in the saddle room using horse rugs as covers. He cleaned it up marvellously and made the place really decent. He scrubbed the floor, blackleaded the fireplace and whitened the hearth.

The men wore corduroy trousers, which were very hard and always had a peculiar smell, especially when they were new, and jackets made of rough brown cloth which was always called 'fushan' though I later found out its proper name was fustian. When they were working they wore shirts without ties, but when they went out at the weekend some wore mufflers round their necks and the smarter ones did put on ties. They all wore black boots, often with leggings for special occasions, but when they were working some tied straps round their legs and others pieces of string, the idea I suppose being to keep their trousers out of the mud.

The men who lived in washed themselves in the back kitchen. When they wanted hot water the youngest one always had the job of taking a can-full from the kitchen copper. As they were all local men they went home each weekend for a change of clothes and I suppose if they wanted a bath they must have had it then as they never did at the farm.

I once remember my elder sisters, Annie and Ada, playing a joke on the men who slept in the house. These men always left their boots and caps at the bottom of the ladder before they went to bed. So one night after they had gone to bed my sisters took their caps and stuffed them under the copper fireplace. My mother knew nothing of this, and next morning lit the fire as usual, burning them all. My father was never told of this or I am afraid there would have been trouble! The men had a good idea who had taken their caps but they never knew what happened to them. Sometimes we would make an apple pie bed or put a sweeping brush in their bed, and, at Christmas time, a bunch of holly. All these jokes were taken in good part and we had many a good laugh.

FOOD

Food was a most important part of our lives and preparing it took up most of my mother's time. She did vast bakings each day except Sunday, and all the pies and cheesecakes she made would be eaten that same day. I think we ate much better than many people at that time, and visitors who came from Hull were always full of praise for the quality of my mother's cooking. Even if the men who lived in came from the local villages and could go home on Sundays, they still came back to us for their meals, as their families apparently could not afford to feed them in the way we did. We had a cold midday dinner on a Sunday, but anything special we had was usually reserved for the weekend.

Everything had to be done on a big scale. We bought large joints of meat weighing half a stone each, and the butcher delivered to the house weekly. In summer, deliveries would sometimes be made by two butchers. A great deal of meat was eaten and it was even served cold at breakfast time. There was always plenty of bacon, and meat was kept fresh in brine. Sausages were only available at pig-killing time. The men had bread and cheese for their mid-morning and mid-afternoon breaks and we bought large round cheeses as well as Dutch red cheeses. My father always took the head of the men's table at breakfast and dinner and did all the carving and dishing out of the meat and pudding for each man. There was never any choice. The men had to take or leave what was put before them.

In the early days the men had basins to drink from, but not my father. Later these were replaced by pint mugs. Warm milk was always provided at breakfast time and water only at dinner time, although my father stayed behind when the men had left and had tea. We drank very little coffee, but the men did have tea with their breaks and, as a special treat, tea would be given with their evening meal. My father also kept a barrel of beer in the cellar. We made our own beer, which at one time was drunk by the men who were harvesting, but later we went back to tea. My mother also made damson wine, and I remember one year all the corks popping up and hitting the ceiling. There was not much change in the food from one week to another but there was always plenty of meat and plain food, though no fancy dishes. It was only on Sunday night that no meat was provided – only bread and butter and cheesecake pie.

Fruit and vegetables were always very plentiful when they were in season, but not otherwise. Tomatoes were something fairly new. Everybody in the family was very fond of them. They cost 6d a pound and we bought them in Thorngumbald, the village where we went to school. We had very few oranges until my eldest brother, George, began work in Hull; he would go in to the wholesale market in Humber Street and send us a box of fruit. Once I watched one of the farmer's daughters (who went to school in Hull) very proudly peeling and eating a banana in front of me and I felt very envious.

By modern standards we ate a lot of stodgy food and probably too much meat, and there was always brimstone and treacle available. I suppose, too, we did not eat enough green vegetables. We bought no ready-made foods. Bread and butter were home-made (though the latter in the farmer's house) and we ate bread without butter. Biscuits, toffee, lemon curd, ham and pickles were all produced at home, and such luxuries as iced cakes were made only at Christmas time.

I remember the first time we bought Quick Quaker Oats. This was a big improvement as the ones we had used until then took so much longer to cook. There was very little – if any – experimenting with new recipes. The same things were made year after year. All the cooking was done from memory and by instinct and we used no cookery books. I do not think we tried anything new until my elder sisters, Annie and Ada, went out to work and brought back new ideas. My eldest sister, Annie, had been so well trained at home that she was able to take up the post of cook. At one house at which she was cook she was allowed to entertain some friends, and a good display of cakes was put on the table. They were, however, only for show as my sister's employer told her she was not to cut into any of them!

Pig killing was a very busy time and brought a lot of work. A local butcher from Thorngumbald would come early one morning bringing everything that was needed, scalding tub, knives, scrapers and so on. I never actually saw a pig killed but I often watched the butcher scraping all the hairs off the pig he had just killed. A great big copper was filled with boiling water ready for him, and all the work was carried out in the 'steam house', as we called it. The pig looked so clean and white hanging from the roof when he had finished that day, and the next day he came again and cut it up into pieces, hams, shoulders, sides and all the other cuts.

This was the point at which our work started. The first job to be done was always the making of the black puddings. These consisted of blood, milk, groats, salt and pepper, and were cooked in pie dishes in the oven. Then came sausage making. The meat had to be cut up into small pieces and was seasoned with marjoram, salt and pepper, and well mixed before being put through the machine. Very large dishes were used for the meat to drop on to and it was a very tiring job turning the handles of the machine. The skins were slotted on to a funnel attached to the machine, and the meat had to go through the machine and through the funnel; then the skin containing the meat would slide off. It was quite interesting work and I liked doing it.

Pork pies were the next job and it took some time to get these ready for the oven. The crust had to be made in a special way: warm fat and milk were put into the flour and mixed to a stiff dough which was put into tins and filled with minced pork. The tops of the pies were always decorated with some of the dough cut into shapes such as leaves. They always came out of the oven a lovely golden brown and the smell was wonderful.

Brawn was the next thing to prepare. All the bits and pieces of pork which were left after the hams and shoulders had been shaved, together with the pig's trotters, were put into a large pan and boiled for hours until the meat left the bones. The bones were removed and what was left was put into moulds and left to set. The final job was the salting of the hams. These were rubbed well with salt and afterwards laid in salt on the dairy floor for a month.

All that was left for us now to do was to eat pork for weeks! I am afraid we were all tired of it by the time we got through pork pies, sausages, brawns and black puddings. I have often wondered how we managed to keep it eatable for so long as we had no fridge in those days, although the dairy was partly below ground level and was always very cold.

I remember that my father's mother always came to help on these pig-killing occasions. She lived three miles away in Thorngumbald and had to be fetched by horse and trap and she always stayed the night. As our house was fairly small for the number of people who lived in it, we had few visitors who stayed overnight and they were always members of the family. My grandmother[7] always seemed old to me but she was still very active and worked very well.

---

7   Born Hannah Jackson, a member of a large Preston (Holderness) family, in 1839, she married James Gardner in 1861. The marriage was at Sculcoates parish church and both bride and groom gave their addresses as Charterhouse Lane. James signed the marriage register, but she made her mark (though as already mentioned in the text above she later took the *News of the World*.) She died in 1919.

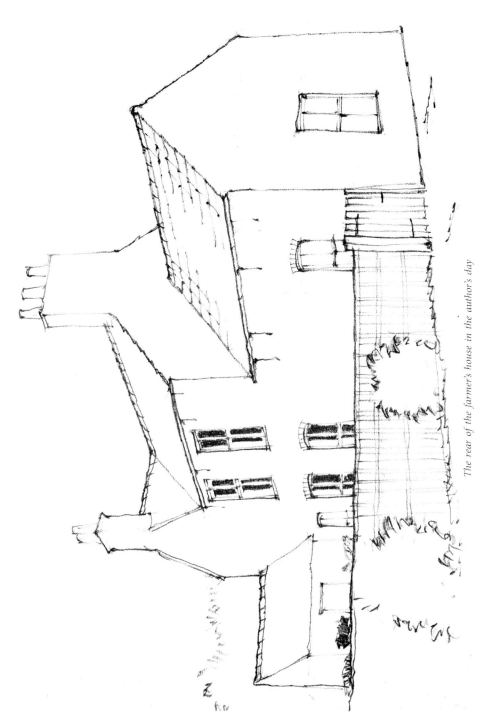

The rear of the farmer's house in the author's day

THE FARM

The farm was quite a large collection of buildings, each of them there for some particular purpose, and as we were out in the country we had to be as independent as possible. It was almost like a hamlet, surrounded by a belt of trees – beech, elm and willow – which had been planted to protect it from the bitterly cold winds which blew from the coast and in which birds were very ready to settle and build their nests.

As well as the farmer's house and ours there were three large granaries, a main one for storing corn, another for corn to be milled, and a third one for cake for the cows and beasts. There were also two stack yards, barns, wagon sheds, a blacksmith's shop, a mill house containing a big mill, a coal house for storing the fuel for the steam engine used on threshing day, pig sties, cow houses, calf houses, and stables with a granary above for the horses' corn.

We kept Shire horses – black, brown and white – which were very big and heavy but usually very quiet. Most of them were bred on the farm and my father used to break in the foals. There was a blacksmith's shop with an anvil, but a man would come from Thorngumbald to do any work that was required. The farm carts were always very noticeable in the fields because they were painted very vividly in yellow ochre. They were always used for funerals – even for important local farmers and landowners.

Barns enclosed the big fold yard which in turn was divided into pens for the milking cows, the small calves, and the bull. Pigs were allowed to roam about amongst the other animals. The bull was only penned up in winter; in the summer it ran with the cows. There was, I suppose, no real breeding plan; things just happened when they did.

I had a terrible fright once. On my way to fetch a bucket of milk from the farm house I turned the corner of a building and came face to face with the bull. It was a monstrous white animal and I have never been so scared in all my life. I dashed up the granary steps nearby for safety – wasn't I glad to find them there! I imagine I just let the bucket drop. In fact, one of the farm men was following close behind the bull to get it back into its pen from which it had escaped so the whole episode ended very quickly without any further harm.

Looking back I now realise that the farming was very wasteful and I can see why so many local farmers later went bankrupt when things became more difficult. Lots of calves died off; they were left to men who were not qualified to look after them properly and did not understand how much cleanliness was needed for them to be kept alive and healthy. Dead calves were often thrown into the paddock and left unburied. Chickens, of course, were allowed to roam anywhere they wanted – it was certainly a very free-range system. No one kept any account of the number of chickens on the farm and you would sometimes come across them dead or dying. There was a great clearing-up before the Constable's agent paid his annual visit to the farm and lunch was always put on for him at the farm house.

Gathering eggs was a very difficult job in these circumstances. There were several chicken houses but the birds would lay in any secret place they could find. We also kept ducks and guinea fowls – noisy birds which roosted in the fir trees in the farmer's garden.

As children we enjoyed collecting eggs for the farmer's wife. It was the custom on a farm for the money from the sale of eggs to be the farmer's wife's pin-money and she would send them to the grocer and have their value set off against the amount she owed him. She did not want any cracked eggs, and any we collected we were allowed to keep for ourselves. Once a visitor to our house who was helping us collect the eggs heard the instructions about keeping the cracked ones, so he made quite certain there were plenty cracked! The hens would lay in place we could not reach. Dozens of rotten eggs would be found between the stacks at threshing time. I do not believe they ever made a penny profit out of their chickens – more likely a loss, it was all so inefficient.

I was more successful with a pen of hens which I kept for a time. As a reward for the help I was giving, the farmer said I could have free corn for some hens of my own, so I could hardly avoid making a profit. My father bought me 12 Black Minorcas. They were beautiful birds and lay massive white eggs. Sometimes when I went to collect them there were more eggs than chickens so some of them must have laid twice a day. I used to take them into Hedon by bicycle, a deep round basket on each handlebar, and a woman who lived there would take them off me to sell at the butcher's shop she and her husband kept in Hull. It was at the end of the First World War when things were scarce and I was able to sell them for as much as 6d each, a terrific price in those days.

SCHOOL

As I look back I feel that the walk to school was not too bad, although we did have three miles to go. We had certain places to pass along the way by which we could judge how far we still had to go. It was amazing how many different birds and small animals such as rabbits and rats we saw. There was even the odd fox. As we passed one of the farms someone would give us a wave and even brought out a few apples for us to eat on our way.

We left home about 7.30 am, often in the dark in winter, and it was usually around 8.40 am before we arrived at the village. Sometimes we had a penny to spend at the local shop and then we made our way to school. Although we lived furthest away from the school we were always the first there! A problem, though, was that I had a friend whose parents kept a shop. She would say, 'You will call on me, won't you?' and I would be made late waiting for her. The attraction, however, was that she would pick a handful of sweets on the way out of the shop for us to share.

I always liked the Infants' school and was very sorry when I had to move higher. The school had three rooms, Infants, Standards 1 and 2, and large room for Standards 3 – 6. Women taught the lower classes but a master, John Wright, the higher one. I enjoyed being in Standards 1 and 2 as we had a very nice woman to teach us. She was smartly dressed and spoke very nicely to us.

Things certainly got worse, however, when I moved into the higher class and had the man to teach us. He can only be described as cruel. He really made life awful and used the cane every day. Not that I got it but once, and that was a mistake when my brother and cousin were talking in class. I was in the middle of them and we were all brought out to the front and punished. I have never been so ashamed in all my life. The master had an awful temper and would just scribble across our papers without reading them and throw them on the floor.

His son and daughters came to the same school and they were not spared in any way. The master's wife came to school twice a week to take the girls for needlework. She was a very nice person and I felt very sorry for her one day as her son was being caned so hard that she had tears in her eyes. What a relief it as to get away from school! We were made to sit up straight with our hands behind our backs; anyone who moved the foot rest under the desk had to sit on it.

He was always getting on to somebody, and he would tantalise anyone who was a bit slow. The boy who sat next to me at school was an awful dunce at his lessons and the master never gave him a chance. The poor boy led a terrible life. I remember his mother coming to the school yard to complain about this ill-treatment while we were all standing in lines waiting to march inside. The master pointed his cane at her as he walked her to the gate shouting, 'Get out!' We stood in our lines terrified. The odd thing is that the boy has since been very successful and has built up a large and prosperous business for his sons to carry on.

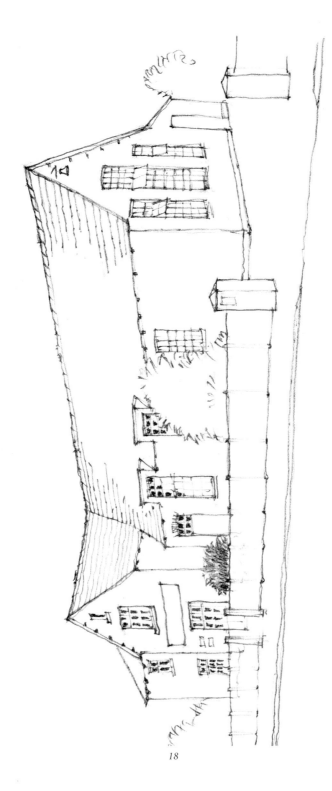

The school

The master found pleasure in taking advantage of anyone who was at all simple. He enjoyed 'April fool' jokes, and once sent a boy into the village for 'a long stand'; of course, the boy had been trained to do as he was told and so he was kept waiting around until it was felt he had been kept standing long enough.

Another habit was to try to frighten us all by telling us that when Peter and he stood at the gates of heaven he would say, 'Get behind me, Satan!' when it was our turn. These things made us long for the day when one could leave school. I reached Standard 5 but I could not say that I enjoyed school at all – in fact I hated it. Although his cruelty was well-known, nothing was really done about it. I believe he was summonsed but got away with it. I believe, too, he once pulled my eldest sister's hair and my father complained; I do not think it ever happened again. In winter it was often dark by the time we arrived home and he would love to pile on the agony by keeping us in, and making a fuss of lighting the gas lights to show us how late we were going to be.

Because of the long walk involved I did not begin school until my seventh birthday. By this time my two elder sisters, Annie and Ada, had left home and gone to work, and my eldest brother, George, who had been very clever at school, had started work on the farm. A brother, Eddie, 18 months older than myself was still at school, and so I had to go along with him.

The first day was really frightening, although the teacher was very nice. She had frizzy hair and I still remember her habit of sucking one of her teeth. Her name was Miss Duffill and we called her 'Duffy Wool'. When it came to dinner time we all went to the cloakroom to get our dinner bags. I had started school after Christmas and, as it was winter, we were allowed to go into the classroom to eat. I was either too shy or did not know this, and stayed in the cloakroom (which we called the Board Room) by myself. I do not think I even attempted to eat my sandwiches – I just stood and did a weep. However, I shall never forget the older girl who came and found me – Ivy Smith. She took me by the hand and let me sit next to her in the classroom so in the future I knew what to do.

The brother who was at school with me was the biggest worry I had. He was a dunce in every way and was always in trouble. It never bothered him, but I was pleased when he left at the age of 12 years to help on the farm.

Although I was not keen on school, I was always pleased if I could attend regularly. The distance meant that on very wet days we were kept at home, or we would have been sitting in wet clothes all day. I never remember the master saying anything directly to us when we had been away, but he would keep making snide remarks, particularly when you had missed work and were not sure what to do.

I did enjoy the cooking and the sewing lessons, particularly as the headmaster's wife used to take us into her house to give us practical lessons in cookery. What a relief it was to go into the headmaster's house on a Friday morning. Usually we went at half past ten and stayed the rest of the morning. Sometimes we would have particular jobs to do such as cleaning the silver or we were taught the correct way to do various tasks, for example, cleaning hair brushes. But usually we helped prepare the midday meal and we got up to all sorts of mischief and had a lot of fun.

I wonder if the headmaster's wife ever realised what we were doing – I liked her very much – she was such a sweet, lovely person – but, of course, she could not be in every room to keep an eye on everybody. When we had to chop almonds to make a cake we each helped ourselves to one, and a quarter of a pound of almonds ended up in the cake

Thorngumbald School, circa 1909

as two ounces. I remember when we were making bread my cousin threw the dough up into the air and caught it. On another occasion a girl chopping suet for a pudding accidentally chopped off a bit of her finger. Later, when we were back at school, the master never stopped talking about the possibility that he might have eaten the piece of flesh in his food. Usually we worked in the daughters' bedroom, not their parents', and we had a grand time trying on their hats and clothes and sampling their perfume. The lessons were really very enjoyable and I learnt some useful things. One small thing which interested me was the fondness of the headmaster's wife for using haricot beans in all hot meat dishes, something we never did at home.

I was always very fond of poetry and I may say I still am. When I was younger, if I saw any poem I liked I would learn it by heart. Sometimes now when I am in bed and cannot sleep I recall many pieces which are quite long. At school I learned the *Wreck of the Hesperus*, of which I was very fond, and also *Horatius,* which had to be recited with all the correct actions. Others we learnt were *Fidelity, Casablanca, Mr Nobody, The Builders,* and there were many more. One I liked was called *Somebody's Mother,* which told the story of a young boy helping an old woman across a busy street. It began:

> The woman was old and ragged and grey,
> She bent with the chill of the winter's day,
> Her feet were wet with the recent snow,
> And the woman's feet were feeble and slow.
>
> She stood at the crossing and waited long,
> Alone, uncared-for amid the throng
> Of human beings who passed her by,
> None answered the call of her anxious eye.

The master was very keen on singing but there was no music to accompany our songs. Instead he used a tuner to get the note, knocking it on the desk and then letting it vibrate – sometimes even putting it on his teeth.

I always liked the songs we used to sing at school. *Hearts of Oak* was always the first in the song book, and others we sang were *Robin Adair, The Lark, Woodland Walks and Dells, Springtime, Fairy Elves* and many more. We always began in the morning with the hymn, *Awake my Soul.*

When an Inspector was due to visit the school it was obvious that the master was very worried. He wore his best suit and the atmosphere was very tense. We always knew when an Inspector was expected. Although we were not tested individually on the day, we had previously prepared special work for him to look at.

The Infants' room had raised galleries, the very youngest children sitting in the bottom row. I remember Miss Duffill's voice now as she tried to train us to move quietly from our places – which was not easy in a galleried room. '*Step* into the gallery!' she would sing out, and if we did not do it quietly enough she would raise her voice and order, '*Back* into desks!'

Living away from the village we never met the teachers out of school, although I think the master was on the Parish Council and took part in village affairs. Miss Duffill had lodgings in the village and the other lady teacher, Miss Fewster, travelled each day by train from Patrington. She was a very nice smart little person always neatly dressed in a long skirt and a white blouse. When the master looked at her through the glass section in the screen dividing their classrooms she used to blush up to her hair roots.

We always wore pinafores at school and I loved getting a new one. Usually we bought them at the grocer's shop in the village but on one occasion I remember my mother's cousin in Derbyshire sending us for Christmas pinafores with lovely crocheted tops. I was very proud of mine, especially when the headmaster's wife admired it and asked me to let her borrow it so that she could copy the pattern.

My sisters and I usually wore boots and black stockings held up with garters and I can remember my mother telling us to 'get a yard of garter elastic' from the village shop. As

25 (b) Thorngumbald U.D. Board School Time Table

Morning — Afternoon

Day	Class	Religious Instruction	9.30 to 10.20	Musical Drill	10.30 to 11.15	11-15 to 12	1 - 1.30	1.30 to 2.30	Drill	2.40 to 3.35	Dismissal
Monday	1		Arithmetic	Object lesson	Reading	Reading	Drawing (Boys)		Writing	
	2		do.		Geography	do.	do.		do.	
	3		Reading	(Nature Study)	do.	Writing	Needlework (Girls)		Arithmetic	
	4		do.		do.	do.			do.	
Tuesday	1			English	Geography	Reading	Writing		Arithmetic	
	2		Do.	do.	Reading	do.	do.		do.	
	3			Writing	Arithmetic	English	Reading		Recitation	
	4			do.	do.	do.	do.		do.	
Wednesday	1			Object lesson	Reading	Reading	Needlework (Girls)		Writing	
	2		do.	Nature Study	Geography	do.	Writing		do.	
	3				do.	Writing	Reading		Arithmetic	
	4				do.	do.	do.		do.	
Thursday	1			English	Geography	Reading	Writing		Recitation	
	2		Do.	do.	Reading	do.	do.		do.	
	3			Writing	Arithmetic	English	Reading		Arithmetic	
	4			do.	do.	do.	do.		do.	
Friday	1			Reading	Writing	Reading	Drawing (Boys)		Singing	
	2		Do.	do.	do.	do.	do.		do.	
	3			Writing	Singing	Writing	Needlework (Girls)		Arithmetic	
	4			do.	(with Infants)	do.	do.		do.	

Registers marked in Red Ink at 9 and 1. Closed in Black Ink at 10 and 1-25.

Class 1. Standards IV V & VI.
I — III
II — II
III — I

Approved at a Meeting of the School Board held on the 15th day of March 1901.
(Signed) M.H. Goundrill, Chairman

Approved on behalf of the Education Department as fulfilling Section 8.11 E.E. Act 1870.
(Signed) W.H. Anstead Inspector
March 21st/01.

Copy. J. Table now in use at Thorngumbald

Donkey cart in Thorngumbald, the names of its occupants unknown

a rule we wore woolly hats of the Tam o'Shanter kind. My mother was very clever at crocheting hats and gloves. My brothers, George and Eddie, wore jackets and knickerbockers which fastened just below the knee, with long woollen stockings and boots. They did not usually have ties, although one of them did later begin to wear stiff white collars with a tie.

We went out so rarely when we were very young that there was no point in having 'best clothes' for special occasions. As we grew older we did have our 'best' things for Sundays; they had to be put away as soon as we had finished with them as it just was not done to wear Sunday clothes during the week. There were no school outings that I remember. Sometimes my mother would keep me at home to help her in the house and the Attendance Officer, who was always known as 'The Boardman', would come miles to investigate why anyone was absent from school. I can never remember anyone being fined, though.

One improvement was that eventually we had a donkey and cart for driving ourselves to school. By this time my two younger sisters, Amy and Norah, had reached the age for starting school and my brother, Eddie, and I were old enough to manage the donkey cart. It was a very cold drive in winter as the donkey was very slow, but it was better than walking.

I usually had the job of harnessing it as my brother hated school and would do anything to get out of going. Hiding his cap or a sudden pain were his favourite excuses. When we arrived at the village we left the donkey and cart at the blacksmith's. For his kindness in letting us use his stable my father would send him a bundle of straw for his pigs. When this happened, the blacksmith would always give us 2d each, which I thought was grand. I used to buy a twopenny Giant Lucky Packet or a Kali Bunker which I found lasted the whole of the three-mile journey. There were no school dinners, of course, and we used to take bread and a hard-boiled egg or sandwiches. When we arrived home there would usually be something hot for tea which had been left over from dinner time. The only drink available at school was cold water. It was a great thrill when I first took a flask of tea. Unfortunately my brother broke the flask the very first day!

The master's life was to end in a way we never expected. Some years later, by which time I had left school, he was found upside down in a barrel of water.

THE FARMING YEAR

On a very lonely farm where winter made life very harsh and difficult it is not surprising that we really looked forward to springtime, only to find that at first it was very disappointing. An east wind seemed to be blowing nearly all the time and living right on the east coast made things worse. But as time passed and the sun began to shine we all felt much better in spite of the cold. Spring is the time of growing, and the most important growing things were the lambs.

What a time we had helping to fetch the sheep to the fold every night and carrying new-born lambs, their mothers walking very close behind. These were put into small pens inside the fold, away from the other sheep for a day or two. My father would sit up all night and attend to them. As a reward the farmer would always give him a bottle of whisky and a ton of coal for doing the extra work which sometimes lasted for about a month.

The sun in spring does not have much heat in it and we had to wrap up well when we walked round the field where lambs and sheep were, looking in the dykes, as very often a lamb would fall in after playing on the bank. I have pulled many a one out of the water and saved its life. The dykes always seemed very full of water: winter had only just ended and there was plenty of water everywhere when the snow had thawed. We learnt a poem about the months of the year and it did not surprise me that there was one line about 'February-fill-dyke'.

On one occasion when I was out gathering flowers on the side of a dyke I saw a most lovely bunch of daisies and reached out to pick them. I overbalanced and toppled over into the black meggy water. Fortunately one of the men was nearby so he helped me out and I went home crying.

We saw very little of the Holderness Hounds as there were too many dykes for fox hunting. Foxes did sometimes stray on to the land from Paull Holme and once a horse ridden by someone in pursuit fell in the Clough and had to be rescued.

In the fields the men were already getting ready for sowing spring corn and the birds were beginning to sing and make their nests. Crows would make an awful noise as they built their nests in the tree tops. It was said that if they built their nests very high in the tree it was a sign that we were going to have a very fine summer.

We always thought of spring cleaning the house at this time of the year, and every room had its turn. Sometimes rooms needed papering and this was a job done by one of the family. Beds were turned upside down and cleaned, curtains were taken down and washed, pictures and vases all had their yearly clean, and for a time the house was really upset. I am afraid my father just hated this upheaval and would take his gun and go out shooting rabbits as there were plenty of young ones about at this time of year.

This meant I had the job of making rabbit pie. It also meant that I had to skin six rabbits, as we used a very large pie dish and I had to make the pie big enough for six or seven men as well as the rest of the family. Rabbit pie was followed by an apple pie or large rice pudding; otherwise the pudding was always eaten first before the main course. The idea was to save the meat and so fill up everybody first with pudding as this was obviously much cheaper!

About 100 to 150 sheep were always kept on the farm and naturally looking after these was quite a big job. Their feet had to be examined quite often and the hooves needed to be cut. Often, too, they had to be doctored for foot rot. Twice a year it was compulsory for them to be dipped with a special disinfectant for scab.

About April or May was the time for the sheep to be washed so that their wool would be clean for shearing. A big tub was needed and it was put at the side of a large dyke which was full of water. One by one the sheep were washed. A man kept filling the tub with water from the dyke and the sheep could hardly walk when they were taken from the tub, their wool held so much water.

But after a day they were all dry and the next thing was the sheep shearing. This was a great occasion which I enjoyed watching. It meant putting down a large sheet which covered the barn floor and kept the wool clean when it was clipped from the sheep. The sheep were laid on a trestle and it was amusing to see how quiet they were as they were being clipped. This was a process carried out by hand until a clipping machine was introduced, a very big improvement on the old method. I enjoyed many hours watching my father and the farmer doing this job and also helping to roll the wool into a bundle as it came away from each sheep. The farmer's wife would come out with some lovely cheesecakes for their lunch and I always enjoyed a piece myself. The wool was later sent away but I do not know where to.

When haymaking started we really felt that summer was on the way. The mowing machine was got ready and the field of grass which once stood upright was soon laid in neat rows. It then had to be left for one to two days to dry and, providing the weather was fine, it was turned once or twice before it was put into hay cocks. It was then brought to the farmstead by horses and wagon and made into a large stack, a job which meant employing extra men.

The smell of new-mown hay was lovely, but sometimes we knew that something was wrong as the smell from the stack was very strong; the hay in the stack had started to heat and it was likely to fire. In fact, I remember seeing one actually burst into flames. I raised the alarm and soon everybody was rushing around. But there was little they could do and it had to just burn itself out. The fire always started in the centre of the stack and was caused by the hay being gathered in too soon.

The next big event was harvesting, which always coincided with our school holidays. When the harvest really started and the binders were got ready for cutting the corn, a number of Irishmen would come for work. Some had been coming to us for years, and as they became too old a son would come, and even a grandson. They usually stayed six weeks and we got to know them well.

The Irishmen slept in one of the granaries, making their bed of anything such as bags and straw. They ate from an old wooden bench and their food was fetched from our house each meal time. It was always a plain diet which never changed, and consisted of baking-powder cakes and boiled bacon, day after day except Friday, when, for religious reasons, they ate plain cakes and perhaps *butter*. Their idea was to live as cheaply as possible. The place in which they ate and slept had an awful smell of strong tobacco and stale food and bedding. I don't suppose they had a wash the whole six weeks they were with us.

One of them had been coming every year and we got to know him very well and often helped him when he was slicing the turnips for the cattle. This man looked after the cows and the pigs and did very little harvesting. His name was Jim. Sometimes we would hide and call out, 'Sunny Jim!':

> The Sausage was a long one,
> The outside was within,
> The inside was a mixture
> Of a man called Sunny Jim!

He used to grow very angry and would shout, 'If I do find you, I'll break your backs for you!'

Irishmen were all good workers but had very bad tempers, and at the weekend they would make their way to the nearest village and get drunk. Then they started violent arguments with each other. I once remember one knocking one of our men to the ground, kicking his head and leaving him on the roadside. As a result, this Irishman had to leave the farm the next day. On Sunday mornings, however, they always went to the Catholic church, which was five miles away.

A field which was to be harvested had first to be 'opened up' and a man went round the outer sides of the field with a scythe so that there was a way in for the reaper. Somebody followed behind making the cut corn into sheaves, and these sheaves were leant up against the hedge. At harvest time when we were on holiday we had to take their lunch out to them in the fields and for this purpose we used the donkey cart in which we carried a large stone bottle of beer (containing about two gallons) as well as their food. This was usually cheese and bread, or currant cakes.

We also went with one of the men when he took a change of horses as it was hard work for them pulling the binders, and the days were long and tiring. We were allowed to ride on the backs of any which were quiet. It was fun sitting so high and their backs were so broad – it was like sitting on a flat table. I remember when some of the horses took fright and ran away with the binder as they were cutting the corn. They went straight through a hedge, leaving the binder and the pole broken. The boy who was driving the horses did so by sitting on the back of one of them. He fell off, and the binder, or reaper as it was called, went right over him cutting him badly, and he had to be taken to the doctor's.

We were always told when a field that was being harvested was almost finished and we had to go with sticks and try and keep the rabbits in the standing corn until only a long strip was left standing. The men would then walk round this strip with long sticks, killing the rabbits as they squatted in the corn. Sometimes they would kill as many as 40 or 50 in certain fields but in others they were not so lucky.

Not all of the fields were harvested by binders. The Irishmen who came over for the harvest would cut a field of mustard with small scythes, using one in each hand and leaving the mustard behind them in long straight rows. Harvesting this crop was very different from any other. The wagons had to be made extra wide with shelving, and a strong brown sheet was fixed across this to catch all the small seeds which fell from the crop as it was being carted to the stack yard. The mustard was then heaped on another sheet and a very long stack was made as the mustard straw was extremely bulky.

By the time the last load of corn was brought to the farmyard and all the men had come from the fields it was usually getting dark or perhaps moonlight. It was then that the men would stand at the corner of the building and give three cheers, 'Hip! Hip! Hooray!' The farmer would bring a bucket full of beer and all the men had a good drink. One or two would start to sing a bit.

I remember one song they used to sing:

> We've gotten all in,
> We've left nowt out,
> But we've left our neighbour
> In and out.
> We've worn out our shirts
> And torn our skin
> To get our maister's harvest in.
> And now we'll give him a cheer
> And perhaps he'll give us some beer!
> And a further, 'Hip, Hip, Hooray!'

We did not have a harvest supper as some did but everyone was glad that the hard work was finished. The Irishmen who had been engaged for the harvest were paid and they soon left for home but the other men who were engaged for the year stayed and carried on with the usual work that has to be done on a farm.

It usually took about four weeks or more to gather all the harvest in. Some of the men could make a most shapely load and the pikes or stacks all stood like soldiers in a row, waiting to be thatched. There was one man who always came to the farm to do the thatching and it was interesting to watch him straightening the straw with a large wooden comb. His knees were wrapped with sacking so that they would not hurt him as he rested them on the ladder, for this was a job which went on for weeks. At the end of the harvest there was a wonderful sight in the two stackyards. There would be eight pikes and about five stacks in one of the yards, and another eight stacks in the second one.

Some of the corn had to be threshed quite soon after harvest as it was needed for winter sowing. It was a great occasion and everything had to be prepared the day before. The great big black engine had to be brought from its shed by horses and it was so heavy it took three of them to pull it. The threshing machine and elevator also had to be lined up near the stack which was due for threshing.

My father had to go to Thorngumbald and engage a number of extra men for these days. Usually these men had to walk three miles to the farm so they had to leave home very early, as work started about 7.00 am. One of the regular men from the farm had to get up very early and start a fire in the engine, as it took some time to get enough steam up to work the threshing machine and elevator. My father always attended to the engine and kept putting shovel after shovel of coal on to the fire. I always liked to see the door open and the great fire roaring inside. A cart full of coal always stood near, as well as a water cart. It was hard work and everyone had to keep busy. All the men were covered in dust and were glad when the day ended.

Martinmas in November was the time when the farm workers' year of employment ended and also the time when new men were engaged to work for the next year. Men who had been working for a year were now paid. As far as I know they were not normally given anything in advance. If they were not staying on for a further year they took their boxes holding their clothes and left the farm. To us in the house this meant a week free from cooking so much as only one man was kept to look after the animals. It was now that we were able to do some cleaning in the big kitchen. The ceiling and walls were painted green and these had to be washed. It was a hard day's work but we had not to bother much with meals so we got on with the job and we felt more or less free for a few days.

Next came the hirings which took place on Martinmas Tuesday when crowds of men and girls would meet in the Market Place at Hedon and wait to be engaged for a year. There were different grades of farm workers – Waggoner, Third Lad and Fourth Lad – and they were paid according to their grade. The highest wage I remember being paid was £60 for the year for a man who lived in with all meals provided. Everyone talked a lot about such a high wage which they had never heard of before, but this was in the later years when men were beginning to drift away from the land and labour was becoming scarce.

My father was paid £28 a month and I made out his bills to the farmer for this amount and for the cost of the food supplied to the men living in. My mother was supposed to get all the money for the food. Once he kept some of it back and I remember her throwing back at him what he had given her.

The girls or women would be engaged in the same way as the men and try to obtain the highest money for their services. The whole process always caused a lot of fun for everybody and many of them were worse for drink. It was their one real holiday of the year. They had money to spend and the men usually bought a new outfit – a suit, boots and leggings. They would shout to one another in the street:

> 'Diz thee stop agin?'
> (Are you staying again?)

And get the answer:

> 'Ay, an' sleep wi' maister!'

The author (seated) with elder brother, Eddie, and eldest sister, Annie

CHILDHOOD

We always looked forward to our six weeks' summer holiday which coincided with harvest time and was always known as the 'Harvest Holiday'. During our holidays we always seemed to have fine hot days and we never wore socks the whole six weeks. As we lived so near the Humber we spent a lot of time on the river bank and used to invite our schoolfriends to come and picnic with us. Sometimes we had a fire and boiled a kettle – there was always plenty of wood left behind by the tide. We hunted, too, for tiny crabs under the chalk stones. Once my father found a conger eel on the bank still alive. He brought it home and it was later eaten.

One Sunday morning my father took us for a walk to the Humber Bank. I was so excited by what I had seen that I could not get my words out properly and I told my mother, 'We saw a rabbit! Was it a hare?' This remark became a family joke and was repeated over and over again. We found many interesting things the tide had left behind, once even the body of a man who had jumped in the river when he was drunk and had drowned. Often cargo lost from ships washed up on the bank, including boxes of butter and tinned milk. Anything of value was supposed to be given up to the coastguard but I am afraid this did not always happen. I remember enjoying the tinned milk on fruit and fruit pies for months.

Every day in the holiday seemed to bring something fresh to do. My brother, Eddie, and I were always together, and most of the time the younger daughter from the farm, Kathleen, whom for some reason we nicknamed 'Babs', was with us. We would walk miles around the farm finding reeds and using a thorn from a hedge to slit them into long fine pieces. When we came to the turnip field we would each have a turnip to eat; one of us always carried a knife for cleaning and cutting them. A favourite game was to rob sparrows' nests, put the eggs in a row on the ground, close our eyes, and hop down the row, breaking as many as possible. It was a wonderful area for seeing almost every type of bird as, apart from ourselves, they were left to nest undisturbed.

Another favourite game which we could only play when it was dark was to go round the straw stacks with a sieve on the end of a fork and slide down the sides, catching birds that had gone to roost for the night. These we fed to the ferrets. When it was dark we played hide and seek round the straw stacks. People were still about because the men worked as long as possible, even in the moonlight.

Harvest was a great time, and we often helped with small jobs. One of these was to fetch a load of tares in the donkey cart to feed to the horses and keep them patient as they stood with a wagon full of corn which was being unloaded. Another time we would fetch a cart load of cattle cabbages for the sheep. One day a very strong wind was blowing and, on our way to the field to get another supply, I, as usual, had to get out of the cart and open all the gates. The wind was so powerful that I could hardly do this and the wind took one gate out of my hands just as my brother, Eddie, was driving through, standing upright in the cart. He was in great pain with his arm and all he would say was, 'It's your fault! It's your fault!' I felt awful about it. Nevertheless we still went for the cabbages, although he was complaining about the pain all the time. When we arrived home and told my mother, we went to find my father, though no one knew how bad it really was. It happened that the vet was on the farm attending to a sick horse, so my father asked him to look at my brother's arm. He was certain it was broken, and my brother was taken immediately to the doctor's to have his arm put in splints. I may add that this did not seem to bother him much – the splints were broken many times. Eddie was always up to something and we often said that he was like a cat with nine lives. When he was quite small he drank some poison and had to be rushed to the doctor. Once he put his foot into a copper full of boiling water while looking for fireworks on a high shelf, and on another occasion he fell from the granary. One day he was sitting on a branch hanging over a drain to show me how clever he was. The branch broke and I was so afraid that I ran home and left him in the water shouting for help and leaving him to be pulled out by somebody else.

Towards the end of the summer we always went to the riverside to collect rock samphire, or 'semper' as we called it. This grew on mudflats and was a little bushy plant, green in colour and edible. We would take big baskets and fill them until they weighed almost a stone, as it was impossible to pull up the plant without any mud attaching to it. Our boots and hands were a sorry mess by the time we had finished.

However, it was well worth it. After it had been taken home and washed many times, the roots had to be cut up and boiled until they were tender. Hot vinegar was poured over the samphire after it had been packed in jars and it was then left to cool. It was then ready for eating. Rock samphire tastes very good eaten with cold meat, and it is sometimes known as 'poor man's asparagus'. The fleshy part slips off between your teeth and the stringy stem is left behind. I have recently seen a film of rock samphire being harvested off the Norfolk Coast, but it is not a particularly well-known delicacy, even in East Yorkshire.

It was now that my mother made the jam for winter, mostly plum and apple, as we had very little soft fruit in the garden. We did go brambling around the hedges and we knew where we would always get plenty. These were made into large bramble cakes, which were delicious served warm and just running with juice. Pickles such as onions, red cabbage and chutneys always came in their turn. These were made in large quantities and stored in very large jars. Toffee making was another favourite with us. It was just made with sugar and treacle. I am afraid it never lasted long as we were a long way from any shops and we got very few sweets.

When we were young we loved our parents to go out, as they usually did once a week to Hedon, so that we were free of discipline. Once they had gone we really played up, dancing on the table and making toffee. As soon as we caught sight of my mother and father returning we hurriedly put the youngest ones to bed to make it appear they had gone at their proper time!

I shall never forget an awful thunderstorm we had one day. It had been a beautiful morning and no one could think it could change into what was an awful storm. My mother and father had gone to one of the villages to do some shopping and my sisters and I were left at home. The afternoon seemed to turn grey after the sunny morning we had enjoyed, and clouds started forming in the skies. From one direction a great black cloud was moving towards us all the time and in the distance we could hear thunder. I never liked thunder and began to feel frightened; my sisters felt the same. It was not long before daylight turned to night and the lightning flashed and lit up everything. We were so afraid that we got under the long table that stood alongside the wall and sat on the hard floor. We thought it would never pass over and we were so glad when an old man who was working on the farm came into the house. He did not say much but it made us feel better just to have someone else in the house.

I do not know how long we sat there but it seemed hours, as the storm kept returning. The three of us wanted to go to the lavatory and I am afraid we all had wet pants by the time it was over. My mother and father were on their way home when the storm broke and were bringing back some scythes for the farm. My father was afraid the lightning would strike them so they were thrown into a dyke and left there. When they arrived they were both drenched and almost as frightened as we had been.

We had a sheep dog called Paddy and many cats. If any animal died, for example, a cat or a bird, my younger sisters would bury it with a full religious service and make a neat grave. There was, in fact, what looked like a well-kept cemetery with rows of tiny graves on the top of which were flowers and small crosses. I should add that this was near the earth closet which was about twenty yards from the house. When dark nights came on we dare not go alone so we took a lantern to show the way and often had a sing-song while waiting for each other.

We played a lot of games and enjoyed ourselves a lot. Tiddlywinks was a favourite game and as girls we were very fond of dolls. There seemed to be seasons when certain games would suddenly become popular with all the children at school – hoops, tops and jacks all went through their periods of popularity. I never really mastered jacks but some of the girls were very expert in picking all the jacks up quickly. At home, too, we would have crazes for particular hobbies; for a time we would all be keenly interested in French knitting, at another time we would all be pricking rag rugs. We loved comics – when we could get them. Once, when my elder sister, Ada, had married, her husband brought us the entire 13 comics that were available, including such favourites as *Tuck* and *Rainbow*.

My eldest sister, Annie, made up some wonderful stories and she told the same ones to us over and over again. Often we were mentioned in these stories and we knew them all by heart. She told us stories in which we all went hunting. My elder brother rode a donkey which would not go fast enough so he took out a pin to make it go quicker. I always rode on a pig and wore a red coat. It was all so real that one day I asked, 'What happened to my little red coat?'

Apart from prayer books and a big family bible (which had entries showing that my father's family originally came from Tivetshall St Mary in Norfolk) we had very few books. My parents were not big readers though my father did like a newspaper. I cannot remember ever hearing much talk about politics apart from my father's threats of what would happen to us if a war broke out between Britain and Germany. Although I now know that this was a time of great trouble in Ireland, I have no memory of any of the Irishmen on the farm ever saying anything on this subject. We were really very isolated from what was going on elsewhere. As far as I know my father always voted at elections but I do not think he ever went to political meetings.

Something which gave us a lot of pleasure was the phonograph. I cannot honestly say that I remember our getting it but I should be about 10 or more when I first became interested in it. The phonograph had a small horn as well as a large one, held by a stand,

and a long black box contained about 40 records. We had many happy times with it but we were not allowed to have it on whenever we liked, only if my father was in the mood for music.

Florrie Ford's songs were all popular with us and a big favourite of mine was called *Red Wing*. A laughing song was also one we put on many times: it always caused us to start laughing and we could not control ourselves once we had started. Nellie Wallace was another singer whose records we played but I cannot recall her songs.

The farmer's house, as it was in the author's day

FRIENDS AND NEIGHBOURS

The only other house at Little Humber was the much larger one of the farmer whose family consisted of his wife, son and two daughters and also an unmarried aunt who made her home with them. They also kept a maid, and, when they could not get one, a woman would come from the next village to help in the house. I often went myself and helped at the farmhouse, just for an hour or two when they could not get anyone else. All the family were very nice to me and it was like going home whenever I went to the house, which was, in fact, every day as I had to fetch a bucket of milk for us to use at home.

The younger of the daughters, Kathleen, was about three years older than me, but we were always good friends and spent much of our lives together. She went to a school in Hull but was on holiday the same time as ourselves. Because of the difficulty of travel she stayed away during the week, lodging with people in Hedon, and we looked forward very much to the week-ends when she came home. I remember one thing she said which always struck me as being very amusing. She had been to Hull and she told me that she did not know what to do so she decided to go and have a tooth out!

The aunt who lived with them, Miss Fahy, was rather a snob and did not like her playing with us as were merely the foreman's children. The mother, however, was a very nice person though a very heavy drinker, something which caused a lot of unhappiness in the family as she would do anything to get a drink. She always liked to go out each Friday afternoon and, as no one else would take her, I did, driving her in the pony and cart. She was, I know, highly delighted with me, for she only had to say where she wanted to go or even whom she wanted to visit and I took her there. When she went with her own family they were always in a hurry to get her back home. I, on the other hand, quite enjoyed the job, and the pony, Snowball, was old and easily manageable.

We would drive over to one of the villages or to Hedon and leave the pony and trap at one of the public houses and go to the shops and just take our time. She would have a few drinks, buy a stock to bring back, and sometimes she wanted driving home, through Paull, where she called at the Crown Inn. I knew the family there and I would go into their private rooms and have a lemonade which the farmer's wife bought for me. Although she became rather merry when she had had a drink she was never offensive. She was always very kind to me. She drank a lot of port and would sometimes ask me to take a letter to a shop in Hedon. As a result I would be given bottles of port which were supplied on credit. When I took her out in the pony and trap she would settle her bill and stock up with more drink. There was at the farm a wooden shed full of casks of bought beer, which we called the canteen. When my father opened up the canteen the farmer's wife would be around with a jug. She also hid bottles in the garden and her sister shared her liking for drink.

We always referred to the farmhouse simply as 'the house'. It was a big rambling house with 12 rooms. There were two kitchens. The first had a large cooking range with a coal fire and a deep pit for the ashes to fall into, which was emptied once a week. It was from this hearth that I first heard a cricket calling; this would happen as the days darkened. The walls were painted green and the floor was covered in black and red tiles, although there was a piece of matting on the floor in front of the fireplace.

A copper at the side of the kitchen range was used on washdays. In one of the corners stood a gun case holding three guns and cartridges, and on the wall at the end of the kitchen hung many lids of different sizes, all of which were polished every week. A long table also stood there. There was also a small table near the window and this was used for most of the family's meals as the dining room was used only on special occasions. The windows of the kitchen had wooden shutters and a ladder from the kitchen led to the room where the maid slept.

The next kitchen was much larger. There were cupboards of many sizes containing dried fruit, pickles, jam and salt. One cupboard was used for dinner services and all the other necessary items for cooking, and one for all the plates and dishes that were used every day. A long table which stood in the centre of the kitchen was used when any parties – such as shooting parties – were held. Hams, shoulders and sides of bacon hung from the beams, and near the wall stood a butter maker which was used only once a week. A small pantry led off this kitchen and contained pans and all the other normal cooking utensils. Eggs were also kept there.

The dairy was down three steps and had a red tiled floor. It was a very cold room and here stood the three shallow lead bowls which were used for setting up the milk until the cream had risen. The cream was taken off the milk every day and collected for a week. It was then put into a churn and, after a lot of turning, was made into butter. The liquid which was drained off the butter was called buttermilk. It had a very sour taste and was used to turn milk into curd. Later, a separator was obtained which took the cream from the milk straight after it had been milked from the cows. This was a big improvement and was the end of the lead bowls. A large meat safe also stood at the side.

The dining room was a very pleasant room looking on to the lawn. The floor was covered with a dark carpet and I was always taken with a glass case containing flowers and small birds which stood on the mantelpiece. I once had my Christmas dinner in this room with the farmer and his daughter; the rest of the family were ill at the time. There were easy chairs and a couch and also a piano in the room.

The drawing room, which was at the other side of the entrance, was nicely furnished but was hardly ever used. There was a very fine staircase which led to all the upstairs rooms which contained the usual bedroom furniture. There was no bathroom but there was a room with shelves on each side used for storing apples.

In front of the house was a lawn, surrounded by rose trees and shrubs. A large weeping willow tree stood in the corner of the lawn and underneath it hung a large wire safe which was used to keep any game or hares until they were 'high' and ready for eating. Once, the farmer was given some game which had to be hung until it was 'high'. After a few days he gave it to the beastman to pluck for him. A bit later the man came and said, 'I've thrown it in the ash pit. It was rotten!'

There were many apple trees and also plums, pears and damsons, all of good quality. At one time there were two greenhouses looked after by a man who was employed to do the gardening, and grapes and tomatoes were grown. The vegetable garden was always well stocked. I always remember what a lot of horseradish grew around the garden – the

Dark Lane, as it was

Paull Holme

farmer's wife was noted for her horseradish sauce which she always provided at the shooting parties' dinners when local farmers from all around came to the farm. This garden was very well kept in the early years but later they seemed to lose interest; there were probably money problems as the gardener was no longer employed and it was left to rot and rubbish.

On the way to the next village the road passed two farms, Auster Grange and Oxgoddes, which have always stayed in my mind, and as we passed them it was interesting to notice how they farmed.

The one on the left of the road, Auster Grange, was farmed by a man with a large family and a wife who was very stout and a very jolly person. If you ever passed a remark about it being cold, I remember she would always answer, 'Well, you'll have to warm it then!' This always caused a laugh, and she joined in. Her husband was a small man who told the most ridiculous stories at which you could not help laughing. For example, that he knew of a horse which kicked so hard that it kicked a piece of harness into the air and kept it in the air for half an hour. Every time the harness came down it kicked it up again! He ended every sentence with the word 'like'. Another story he told went: 'One foggy morning, like, when it was thick, like, I heard some wild geese flying over the house, like. I couldn't see them, like, and fired to where the sound came from, like, and you could hear them dropping all way to the river, like!'

There was one son whom you could see ploughing away in the fields and singing to himself as he worked. No one could ever understand the words he sang, which was really nothing more than gibberish. Apparently he sang anything that came into his mind. They seemed to have very poor crops of corn, but they also kept cows, and made butter to send to the market. Their cows always grazed the road sides and they always kept a Jersey cow amongst the others as this was supposed to give extra good milk. At Christmas they dressed quite a number of geese and chickens for the market. They would take all the mats up in the kitchen and all the members of the family had to do their share of plucking. They kept at it all night so that only one clearing-up was needed. They were a happy family in their way and had nick-names for each other. I remember a few, such as 'Bluey', 'Chop' and 'Matta'.

The farmhouse at the other side of the road, Oxgoddes, was a large square place and it was very rare that you saw anyone as you passed. My mother once told me that she lived there as a servant and that one night someone came to steal all the chickens. She heard an awful noise, so she got a gun and opened the window and fired a shot and frightened the men away.

Not far from this farm on the way to Paull was a very dark lane. In fact, it was known to everybody as 'Dark Lane'. Trees grew thick on either side of the road and, even in daytime, it was very depressing going through it. It was supposed to be haunted and many are the times I have been frightened coming home in the dark and hearing an owl call out. Weren't you glad to get through the lane! It was said a man broke his neck as he fell from his horse and this caused it to be haunted.

Further along the road you came to Paull Holme, an old tower. It was covered in ivy and when it was last used no one seemed to know. I went to the top of it one day. It had winding steps and you went round and round until you came to a flat roof. The door to this tower was always left open and cattle in the same field used to hang about it. The story was told that one had been very curious, went in and climbed to the top and, being unable to get back, jumped over the low wall and killed itself.

Near to the tower was a pump. It was fed by a spring and was the place from which we had to fetch our drinking water by watercart. This held enough to last about a fortnight and was only to be used for drinking as it was too precious to waste on washing or cleaning. Our own water at the farm was considered good enough for that.

Further along the road you came to Paull church. It is in this churchyard that my father, mother and sisters are buried and most of the farmer's family, too. The church was old and very beautiful inside and I attended it many times. It stood on a hill outside the village so that people had quite a climb to attend services but there were many faithful people and the vicar was a well-liked person.[8] He also took services at Thorngumbald and I often passed him on his way as he travelled by bicycle. He often

---

8   Rev J T Hutton.

Paull Church

39

Main Street, Paull

visited my home at the farm and he would stay and talk quite a while. On my twenty-first birthday he gave me a prayer book which I still have.

Further into the village of Paull was an old lighthouse with a house attached to it. I was friendly with the family who lived there and I once stayed there after I had been to a dance. This lighthouse[9] had not been in use for a great length of time but it still attracted people and they would take photographs of it. There was also another lighthouse on the bank of the river further away from the village. This was still in use. There was a Battery, too, overlooking the Humber. Territorials used to train there before the war, and when the war started men were stationed there all the time.

I knew most of the people in Paull and really one could call it a small fishing village as most of the men always wore navy blue jerseys and seaboots and went out into the river for fish and shrimps. They were noted for their shrimps and many are the times I have cycled to fetch them for tea – they were always fresh and I often waited for the boats coming in with them. The people had to fetch their water from the pump outside the village and it was a usual sight to see them carrying two buckets with a yoke on their shoulders to lighten the load.

Not far from the lighthouse was a large tin hut which was used for the social events which took place. I remember going there for the Coronation tea and sports and we were each given a mug with King George V's and Queen Mary's head on it.

At the other end of the village was an old museum. I never went into it but I know that the person who kept it was called Rabbit Nanny, who hawked rabbits on the streets of Hull.[10]

I was so used to hearing only people talk with broad Yorkshire accents that I never thought there was anything peculiar about it and very few local sayings have stuck in my memory. I remember my father always called the Russians the 'Rooshans', and Chichester Constable was known as 'Teachester'. When anyone wanted to ask who owned something the question they asked was, 'Whoze owz it?' If anything was very untidy we said it 'looked like Howden Fair!' I suppose Howden Fair must have been a bit of a shambles. Anything slippery was described as 'slape'; people usually put an 'h' in 'treacle' and called it 'threacle'. There was an extra 'r' in 'ir-ron'. Boots were 'bee-ats'. The food and drink taken out to the men working the fields at haytime and harvest was known as their ''lowance', and anybody miserable was said to be 'dowly'. There must be hundreds of other local words and sayings we used but they were so much taken for granted that it is difficult to recall them.

---

9   This lighthouse was built 1836 but became redundant in 1870 when two new lights, known as Thorngumbald Clough Lighthouses, were built further down the river.

10 My mother originally wrote: 'She was supposed to have kept rabbits in a drawer but I don't know if this story was true.' This appears to have been a rural myth. The truth is that she was a Miss Jenkins, a rabbit hawker in Hull, whose voice was so powerful that it is claimed she could be heard in Barton on Humber. Her skeleton is in Fort Paull Museum.

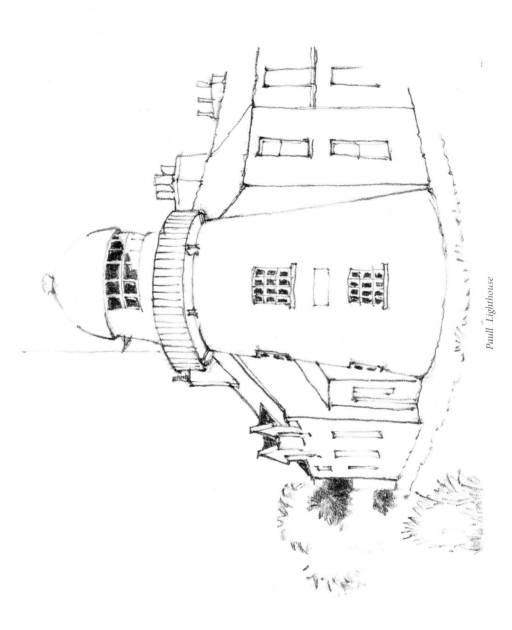

Paull Lighthouse

RED LETTER DAYS

Like everyone else at the time, we took much more note of the seasons and made much more of religious festivals and special events than people do today. For example, we always made a pricked rug in Lent. Of course, we marked Shrove Tuesday by making pancakes, and later celebrated 'Legging Down Day', on the afternoon of 'Oak Apple Day'.

Though we were not Catholics, we were strict about eating fish and having no meat on Good Friday; on this day of the year even the farm men had to go without their usual meat. My grandmother always made Carling peas in Lent. These were baked in an oven with fat and turned greyish-brown. We always kept Good Friday, but did not regard Easter Monday as a holiday. Although I have since heard that it was the custom for farm workers to visit their homes on Mothering Sunday, half way through Lent, our men never did. In fact, it is only in recent years since people started making a fuss about Mother's Day that I have heard about this custom. There were always Easter eggs but they were not usually chocolate ones. Instead we had ordinary eggs which were coloured by being hard-boiled in a pan of water containing onion skins. It was the custom to wear something new at Easter and we tried to do this as far as possible, sometimes wearing a new dress for the first time.

Living on a farm meant that we had to be very careful on Bonfire Night as there were so many stacks of straw about. As a result we had to go away into a field but this did not stop us having great fun. There was always a big heap of thorns left for us and we made a Guy Fawkes from an old pair of trousers, stuffed with straw. A turnip was used for his head and, after scraping out the inside, we cut out eyes and mouth and put a candle inside it which was lit only on Bonfire Night, when it looked rather gruesome and frightening in the dark. The most difficult part was to get a jacket to fit on to the trousers and keep the legs secure, and we always ended with everything coming apart. We never had many fireworks, usually just sparklers, though the men let off bangers. The bonfire was the really important thing and the more things we could throw on to the fire the better we liked it. Our parents did not usually come to the bonfire as it had to be built in a field well away from the hay and corn stacks. I can only remember them coming once when the farmer had a bonfire for his daughters in the farm yard. He put big empty beer barrels on the fire and I remember the great noise they made as they cracked and burned. A Guy Fawkes had been made and he sat on the top of the bonfire in a chair.

As we were so far out in the country we did not have the opportunity to play the jokes on Mischief Night (4 November) which we heard about from our friends in the villages. Taking gates off their hinges was one of the most popular practical jokes, and another was removing the tin lavatory pans from under the seats of the outside earth closets.

The high spot of the year was, of course, Christmas. Many months beforehand we started our preparations. My mother always made a large cake and we helped with the fruit, stoning the raisins and cutting the candied peel, washing the carrots and doing many other jobs. The result was a lovely cake which was stored in a tin after brandy had been poured over it. The Christmas puddings were also made some time before Christmas. It was quite a day when the mixing took place. A great big bowl was needed as the puddings were as large as footballs, everyone was allowed to have a stir and make a wish, and several silver threepenny pieces were mixed in along with the currants, raisins, peel and carrots. Other ingredients added were half a pint of ale, milk, eggs, suet and flour. I know they tasted grand!

The puddings were next put in linen cloths and tied, but no basins were used. They were then popped into the copper, where they were left to boil for many hours. The water had to be kept boiling all this time or the pudding would be sad when eaten, and it was a hard task keeping the fire under the copper burning well. When they were cooked, the puddings were hung up from the wooden beams in the kitchen. They were all the better for keeping and would not be boiled up again until Christmas Day.

Excitement grew as the time got shorter. Although we received only one gift each, on Christmas morning our stocking was always full, with an orange, an apple, nuts, a comic paper, and always a piece of coal for luck stuck in the stocking toes. It was so much better if we had snow for I always thought everything looked so beautiful and, then again, it made so much fun for us. We always had a snowball fight which ended up with one of us crying.

A few days before Christmas we always received a large box by post from my mother's aunt and cousins who lived in Derbyshire, and this was a great treat. It contained dresses, pinafores, stockings and other items of clothing all made by hand. I do not remember us getting very many Christmas cards but I do remember my father getting a goose by post inside of which was a bottle of whisky. We always had a Christmas tree and decorations on the tree as well as hung in the house. I remember us once having a big storm just before Christmas Day. My mother had made bread which had been placed in front of the fire to rise when a gust of wind blew the chimney pot off, sending soot all over the bread and the kitchen floor. We were all so upset about this and thought that our Christmas was ruined, but after everyone had helped to clean the soot away things were soon better.

Christmas Eve was an exciting time and there were still a lot of things to be done. There were dozens of mince pies to be made, as well as buns and cakes. We went to bed early on Christmas Eve even when we knew who filled our stockings, but it was the surprise we were waiting for in the morning. Sometimes we had a visit from carol singers who came three miles from the nearest village, and what a treat that was. My mother always fetched a large dish of mince pies out for them and a drink. Some had a drop of whisky and the young ones coffee. We also gave them money for the church and, after us all wishing each other a Happy Christmas, they left for some other odd farms. I always admired them so much walking all that way to sing carols.

We were all up early on Christmas morning for there were such a lot of jobs to be done – fires to get going under the copper as the pudding needed to be boiled once again and fires in the kitchen so that the oven would be hot and ready for the meat to go in, as everything we had was on the large side and needed plenty of time for cooking. I do not think we ever had a turkey but there was always a large leg of mutton or a choice big piece of beef followed by the Christmas pudding.

The farm men still had the horses and cattle to attend to, but otherwise they had a

Thorngumbald Show

leisurely day. They ate the same dinner as we did, but, even though it was Christmas Day, my father took the head of the men's table and my mother and the rest of our family sat at a separate table.

The postman came late on Christmas Day and was always the worse for drink, as everybody would give him a drink as he delivered their cards, and by the time he got to our house, which was his last call, he was almost helpless. I do not know how he managed to get home. At other times he was a very nice man and I often brought the mail for him if I happened to be in Thorngumbald to save him the journey down to the farm. There were three farms quite near to us and I would bring their letters at the same time. Some would get a daily newspaper by post, which meant that, unless someone helped him out, he had to come a long distance every day and it was usually ten o'clock by the time he reached us.

One day I had gone into the village with the donkey and cart to fetch the groceries and I went to the Post Office for the morning letters. It was a very windy day and, when the postman gave me the letters, I put them on the seat and sat on them. As I was nearing home I thought I would see who they were addressed to, and in doing so, I noticed one was to Miss Fahy, the aunt from the farm. It was then that a gust of wind took it out of my hand and away it went. I stopped the donkey cart and looked in the dykes and at the side of the road and all around but could not find it. I felt really upset and decided not to say a word to anyone but I have often wondered since what that letter contained and whether it was a proposal of marriage. I still wonder to this day – could I possibly have ended a love affair?

OUTINGS

I always looked forward to going out, and our visits anywhere were great occasions which we talked about for months afterwards.

We were always taken by our parents to the Annual Show and Races in Thorngumbald. This was a big occasion for us all, as the horses and wagons were dressed up for the day and everything made clean and bright. A horse with a young foal would be taken from the farm to be shown. I was most interested in the races and my father entered me for the girls' 80 yards handicap race each year. I always won something. Once I won the first prize – a really nice teapot stand, with violets painted on the base and a silver band surrounding it – and another time I won a workbasket.

I remember going to the show for the first time. I was so afraid of the brass band. The men had put their instruments down on the ground and the big horns pointing towards as we stood around in the show field made me feel that they were cannons and would fire at us. I kept pulling at my mother's skirts, edging away all the time. I also recall one year when we were all nearly ready to start for the show and I had a very nice pink dress which I was going to wear. When my mother went to the dresser for it there was no dress to be found and it was never seen again. We always suspected that it as taken by a woman who had come into the house to help my mother. When she met us at the show the first thing she said was, 'Why isn't Alice in her dress?' I do not remember what I wore except that I was very sad about it and it spoilt our day.

There was also an annual outing to Withernsea. My mother would take us on this trip and we had to be in Thorngumbald by 7.00 am, which meant leaving home at 6.00 am. In the village there would be two or three wagons and horses ready, all done up with brasses and ribbons. Every wagon or rully – seats were put on them for the passengers – was full with mothers and children and it was a great success.

It was a slow ride and we seemed ages getting there, so excitement would mount. We would arrive before midday and spend most of our time on the sands. There were donkeys, a Punch and Judy show, and I think there were pierrots – there certainly were in later years. You were supposed to pay for the performance by putting something in a collection, but a lot of us sneaked away before we were approached. The last hour we went round the shops and always brought something home as a souvenir. I once bought a little doll in a bath and, of course, we never came back without a stick of Withernsea rock. We would leave for home about 6.00 pm and what a joyful ride it was. We would sing and laugh and on this occasion did not mind how long it took us to get back. Usually it would be about 10.30 pm by the time we reached the village and my father would be there to meet us with the horse and trap and we arrived back home about 11 o'clock or so, really tired out.

My mother was a real churchwoman and always liked us to go to Sunday School, even though it meant a walk of over two miles to Paull church. I am afraid we did not go

Withernsea

every Sunday and did not win any prizes for attendance but we always went to the yearly party which was a great occasion for us. There was a lovely tea provided and we had games and so on. But there was always that long walk home again and I often wished that I lived in the village instead of on the farm.

One odd thing was that I was not baptised until I was seven when I was taken to be christened at the same time as my two baby sisters. I suppose it was neglected until then because of the distance.[11]

Later, by the time we had left school, we all had bicycles. This was a big improvement as we were able to get out much more easily, so we joined the church and also the choir at Paull. There was a choir practice every week and, after we had been confirmed, we went to Communion quite often. I was confirmed at Sproatley Church by the Bishop of Hull. Only three of us went from the nearest village, Thorngumbald, and we were driven there in an open horse-drawn carriage by Mr Sammy Fisher, a gentleman farmer whose wife was a great churchwoman. In the later years there were choir outings to the seaside and we went by charabanc each summer for a day at either Bridlington or Scarborough.

My mother was very strict about Sundays and did not like us to sew or play games. She attended church as often as possible and walked there many times, sometimes getting up at six o'clock on a Sunday morning to attend early Communion at Paull church.

We always sang an anthem at Harvest Festival and this needed a lot of practice, but

---

11 I have left this uncorrected because it shows the fallibility of memory. Although distance from the church sometimes meant that baptisms were delayed and two children baptised at the same ceremony, Paull Parish Register indicates that my mother was baptised on 24 January 1904, a month after her birth on 19 December 1903. One suggestion is that as a small child she was present at a younger sister's baptism when the vicar gave her a blessing so she would not feel left out, but understood by her to be her own baptism.

we enjoyed it all as it meant being with other people and making friends. For the festival the church was always nicely decorated with corn, fruit, flowers and vegetables, and the night it took place was a great event for us. When the service was over we all stood around talking for a time with our friends and neighbours before beginning the journey home. Our parents drove home in the trap, but when we were old enough we rode our bicycles.

The service was always held on an evening during the week and we usually biked home in the moonlight. At that time, of course, the Harvest Festival was something very important for the farmers and their workers and, as far as possible, it was held when all the harvesting in the district had been finished, not like today when the service is fixed weeks ahead whatever the weather. I always felt better for going out and meeting people but the journey home was always a bit of a drag and took the edge off the pleasure. My father was not a regular churchgoer himself but there were never any objections to us going out if the reason for the outing was to attend church. Once, after a Harvest Festival I remember him saying, 'We'll have to go to church more often,' but he never did. The deaths of my two sisters, Ada and Norah, at the end of the war had a great effect on him and he became much more concerned about the church.

My father rarely went to market but he always attended Beverley Races and later, when he had retired, he was able to visit racecourses further afield. When he went to Hull he put up his horse at the Shakespeare inn in Hedon and travelled the rest of the way by train. On only one occasion do I remember him driving all the way through to Hull – when he went to meet my brother, George, when he was on leave from the army during the First World War.

There was a very big fair in Hull every year in the autumn but we went very little. I do remember going once when I was young but it was with my older sisters. We met one of the men who worked on the farm and he took me on the roundabouts. There were fancy horses which went up and down as the roundabout turned and the steam organ played tunes. On one occasion my eldest brother, George, who was then living in Hull, arranged to meet my mother, my elder brother, Eddie, and myself so that he could take us to the fair. This was such a treat. We left home in the morning to catch the train, did some shopping in the large stores and then visited my grandmother (that is my mother's mother). The visit to Hull was a very rare occasion for my mother as she went out from the farm very little – at times there could be over a year between such outings. Her mother could not understand how she could lead such a life and her sisters were in an awful state about it, blaming my father as they had little use for him. My mother always ended by saying that it was her children who kept her from running away. However, we enjoyed our visit and stayed to tea with my grandmother. Then we left to meet my brother when he finished his work. It was grand to be outside with lights everywhere, so different from our roads at home which were always so dark. One thing always made me feel sorry for my mother. Her feet hurt so much when she was in town, and on this occasion she had to buy a pair of sandshoes as the shoes she had put on were so painful. The problem was that she always wore soft shoes at home and the pavements were too hard for her.

We arrived at the fair and went round all the stalls, had a ride on one or two things, saw all the wild animals, a big snake I shall never forget, and a large elephant standing oddly behind a small gate. But all the bright lights were wonderful: this was the thing that really impressed me. The time soon went by and we had to be thinking of catching

The long road (now called Newlands Lane) leading to Little Humber

a train home. We went to the nearest station, Botanic, my brother saw us into the train, and, we thought, on our way home. It was not so, however, for when we heard the other people who were in the same carriage talking we soon realised that we were on the Hornsea train, not the one to Withernsea we needed to take us to Hedon. We got out at the next station, explained to the station master what had happened and had to wait for a train to take us back to Hull, only just managing to catch the last train home.

When we arrived at Hedon station the horse and trap which was supposed to meet us had gone and this meant we had to walk five miles. It was past midnight but we started to walk. Now, didn't I long for those bright lights we had left behind! We arrived home about two o'clock in the morning and found my father and the rest of the family in bed. Of course, they could not understand why we had not come before. It was the rather sad end of an exciting day and, oh, how I wished that my mother's feet didn't hurt her!

I can remember once taking a short cut on our way to Hull Fair by cycling to Marfleet, leaving our bicycles at a café there, and then travelling into Hull by tram. To reach Marfleet we went through Paull and on to Salt End. There was no industrial building there then, just a stretch of open grassland and, as the modern road and bridge were still unbuilt, we had to cross Hedon Haven by a rough wooden bridge made of uneven planks.[12]

Getting anywhere was always a big problem in our lives, and winter made it even more difficult. We looked forward to any special event, a dance or concert, in one of the nearby villages. We visited Hull at times when we needed shoes, coats and dresses. We did make some of our own clothes and during the winter nights we used to knit.

Going to Hull was a full day's outing. We left home early to catch a train at Hedon five miles away and then travelled another five by train, and by the time we had done our shopping and perhaps visited a relation we had to think about coming home again. I remember we always bought a new record for the phonograph and I always got a songsheet to bring home. I always came home, too, with a headache after being among crowds of people. It was all such a change from the quiet life we were used to, but it was worth it.

Although the winter seemed to last a long time, there was the advantage that more dances were held then in the local villages than in the summer. Music at dances in Thorngumbald was provided by a pianist. In later years a violinist also played – I think he came from Hull. Eventually there were two violinists and towards the end of our time at the farm we even had a small dance band, including drums, for the village dances. They all played very well and we were very happy with everything.

Once a fancy dress dance was being held, so my brother, Eddie, younger sister, Amy, and I decided we would make our own outfits and go. It was such fun. I went as the Queen-of-Hearts and won a prize. My dress was white with small red hearts round the hem, and there was a large heart at the back and front. I had small hearts on my shoes, and a red band round my head with a heart on the front. Such things as these all helped to make life more cheerful and I went to many dances after that, even cycling six or seven miles in the dark and wet weather and thought nothing of it. There was always my elder brother or even someone from the family who lived near us going too, so I always had company – and how we enjoyed being together, laughing and talking as we rode our cycles home at 2.30 am.

---

12 A bridge was built when a new road from Salt End to Paull was opened c 1930.

We dare not complain of being tired the next day for that would have made it difficult the next time we wanted to go out but, oh, how the bed did pull in the mornings! When the shout came for me to get up I would sometimes reach out and move the chair at the side of my bed to make some noise and give the impression I was up! There was always the problem of obtaining permission to go anywhere. If I approached my mother she would say, 'Ask your father,' and I would stand nervously behind his chair plucking up courage to ask him. Even this was not always the end of the matter, as he would often reply, 'Why? What does your mother say?'

We only took a newspaper at the weekend and, as there was no wireless in the early days, we had little news of what was going on outside except what we heard from the postman or anyone coming to do some work on the farm, such as the blacksmith who came often to shoe the horses. Of course, someone was often sent to the village to bring back some groceries. This was my job very often and I enjoyed the break from farm life, if only for an hour or so, and as my grandmother, aunts and cousins lived in Thorngumbald I always paid them a visit and heard all the latest news.

VISITORS AND SPECIAL EVENTS

My grandfather, James Gardner,[13] came from Norfolk, from a village called Tivetshall St Mary near Diss. I have never discovered exactly when or why he moved up into East Yorkshire, but I think it likely that he and his brothers came to get better jobs than they could obtain back home. It is possible that they came to work on the railway but I am not sure about this. In any event, he settled down here, as did his brothers, and he married my grandmother – a local girl – in 1861.

He was a small man and very bent and always walked with a long stick. He sat many hours in his armchair smoking his pipe and used to spit into a small round spittoon which was filled with sawdust and stood on the floor near his chair. He never bothered about money and left everything to my grandmother to see to. You never heard him complain and he spoke very little, but he never lost his Norfolk accent. Although he seemed too old to do anything, he did ride a three-wheeled bicycle and came to visit us. He kept a pig in the sty and was very fond of pigeons which he kept in a cage in the back yard. I don't think he had many illnesses and he was 79 when he died.

My grandmother, Hannah Gardner, was a regular attender of the village chapel and she always wanted us to go too, but my mother had brought us up to attend the Church of England. I did go to chapel once with my cousins but I never felt that I had been to a place of worship. It was so different from a church service. Even the preacher was full of jokes and all the hymns we sang seemed to be jolly. I do not remember telling my mother I had been to chapel for I am sure she would not have liked it.

My grandmother was never seen without something on her head, a bonnet when she went out, and, inside the house, a 'dust-cap' made of cotton materials through which a piece of elastic had been slotted to keep it secure on her head. I remember how she always pronounced cabbage as 'cabbish', and one of her sayings was, 'Have some more cabbish, bairn.' She always kept a tin of condensed milk in her pantry and I loved to go and help myself to a secret spoonful. I supposed as children we had such a craving for very sweet things because we had so few.

My grandparents talked a lot about their pension which they thought was a wonderful thing. Like a lot of local people they called it their 'Lloyd George'. I can never remember my grandfather having regular work. My grandmother was continually complaining about 'rates and taxes' which she thought were far too high. This always puzzled me as

---

13 James Gardner (1839-1911) was the son of William Woods Gardner (1810-42) and grandson of John Gardner, farmers of Tivetshall St Mary, Norfolk. Presumably the poor state of Norfolk's rural economy and the improved wages available in Yorkshire led to the move. John Henry Gardner, my mother's father, was born 23 September 1868 at 7 Charlotte Terrace, Beeton Street, Southcoates, his father James' occupation given as 'Rulleyman'. When and why the move came into Holderness is not known.

I am grateful to local historian Sheila Gardner of Thorngumbald, who has done extensive research into the Gardners' Norfolk roots.

I imagined she was talking about taxi-cabs! She talked a lot, too, about the royal family, for whom she had great respect.

When the First World War came she could never understand what food rationing meant. She would ask me to fetch her half a pound of sugar. The shopkeeper would send me back with a message that she had already had that week's ration. She could not accept this. 'Tell him I can't manage,' she would say. 'I must have another half pound.' When my grandfather died all of us children were made to go upstairs to see him. It was the first time I had seen anyone dead and I think it was quite wrong to make children do this.

My grandmother's brother, George Jackson, was a local preacher and he would come from Preston to preach at the chapel in the village. To do this had to cycle six or seven miles and always brought his lunch with him until a certain event happened. During one service at which he was preaching he was trying to impress the congregation with some point and said, 'This is as true as my lunch is hung on that door!' After this he was always asked to stay to lunch with one of the people who attended the chapel. On one occasion my grandmother was leaving the chapel when she was knocked down by a man riding a bicycle. She was badly shaken and bruised but otherwise she got over it and lived to the age of 79.

We had many aunts, uncles and cousins but we saw them very little as they lived in Thorngumbald three miles away – and some as far as 20 miles away. Until we got bicycles when we were older we had to walk if we ourselves wanted to go out visiting. During the winter we had very few visitors but I always remember the visits in the summer of an uncle who lived in Hull. He was a jolly fellow and caused us to laugh a lot. He always went away loaded with fruit and anything else that was in season. One of his daughters was keen on having a really sour apple and it delighted us to find one of the worst we could possibly pick to send her. We had, in fact, some really nice apples in the orchard and each member of our family claimed a tree as his own.

One visitor we thoroughly enjoyed was my Uncle Billy – in fact, my father's uncle, who came to Yorkshire on a visit from Norfolk which lasted many months. As he was on a pension, I suppose he could afford to do this. He was a jolly old man and we always laughed when he spoke because his Norfolk accent seemed very strange to children who were used to the Holderness dialect. He was always willing to help if he could, and would wash the dishes for my mother when he visited us, something very unusual for a man to do in our home.

He seemed to be able to sing about anything and I always remember him coming home with us in the donkey cart singing:

What a lark we had in the park,
Riding in a donkey cart.
The missus was out and she started to shout,
We'll play the game over again!

Most of the time we had to make our own fun and games, although there were some people who came down to see us fairly regularly. My father had made friends with some fish merchants in Hull, I don't quite know how. Sometimes they would come in a horse and trap from Hull and there were usually four men, all of whom seemed so fat. It was always a Sunday when they came and my mother had to cook a special meal for that day. They always gave my brother some money before they left but their visit did not really interest me.

There was another family, however, whose visits I enjoyed much more. They also came at the weekend and really enjoyed going for a walk with us. They were also fish merchants from Hull, but those who came were the female members of the family. I always remember how well dressed they were in fur coats and lovely dresses but I could always smell fish when I was near to them. My mother enjoyed their visits also, as it was company for her. Although it made extra work, we knew they really enjoyed coming and were grateful.

Each week they would post a card to us, just saying, 'We have sent a basket of fish today. Please collect', which meant it had to be picked up at Hedon Station, five miles away. Believe me, it was a very big basket full of large cods, haddocks and smoked haddock, and often a box of kippers which tasted lovely, not at all like any we bought from the shops. So, although we lived out in the country, we had far more fish than most people and were not really typical of other farms in the area.

These visitors travelled down to see us in a car, I think the first that ever came to our house. It seemed very large with plenty of room inside. One of the ladies always drove it and this itself was a very unusual thing at a time when there were very few cars to be seen. Once a parson came along with them. He had brought a bottle of wine and we all had a wonderful feast.

It was a lonely area for strangers and few came out there except for some definite purpose. During the First World War, when for the first time there were a lot of strangers billeted in the area, I was stopped one foggy night by two men who asked me to direct them to the nearest public house. I told them to take the first turning to the right, which led to Thorngumbald. I have often wondered since what happened to them, as I later realised I had made a slip of the tongue and should have said, 'Take the first turning to the left!' The road I sent them down led eventually to Stone Creek, a very lonely spot, so I only hope they asked somebody else before they got as far as that.

Occasionally there was some excitement. We seemed to have a lot of gales during the winter and on one occasion during the night a ship was wrecked in the river, the men jumped overboard, got to the bank and, seeing a small light which was in one of our windows, made towards it. They knocked us up and we made a big fire in the kitchen and dried their clothes and fed them. Next day a news reporter came down and the story was published in the weekly paper.

In later years seaplanes often came down on the river bank and they had a place they used on the other side. We always went to see what had happened and I remember getting in one of the planes just to say that I had, in fact, been in a seaplane. These were always taken away by road on a large lorry. The most famous incident of all was that of the R38 which I remember well.[14] It was a most beautiful day and the men on the farm were busy stacking. We saw a big airship gliding through the skies, the sun shining on it making it look like a long silver fish. We watched it for some time as it did not appear to be going very fast and, as we watched, it suddenly seemed to break into two parts. We could not see it enter the water as it as over the river and getting further away all the time, but we knew that disaster had taken place and it made us feel very sad as we knew that many lives would be lost and it would mean sorrow for many. I later held a dance in aid of the dependants and raised £34 and I received very nice letter from the organisation thanking me.

---

14 The R38 crashed into the Humber in 1921 with the loss of 44 lives.

Another event was one I would sooner forget. A short time before she was married, my eldest sister, Annie, came home to make all the arrangements which were needed for a wedding. My mother made the cake and iced it, and as our house was on the small side, the reception after the wedding was to be held in Thorngumbald Village Institute. The banns had to be called out in the parish churches of the bride and bridegroom, but there was a misunderstanding about this, and only the bride's banns were read out in her parish, Paull, not the bridegroom's.

It was a lovely day for the wedding and I was one of the bridesmaids. We went to the church by horse and carriage, and we all walked calmly into the church where the bridegroom, who had come from Hull, awaited us. The vicar came from the vestry and asked the bridegroom for his certificate to show that the banns had been called in his parish church. He looked amazed and said he had none. 'Well,' said the vicar, 'I am afraid I cannot marry you.' I shall never forget the occasion. My sister started to cry and we all turned away wondering what we could do. As the reception was arranged and everybody waiting for us it was a quick decision: the reception must go on as arranged.

I sat in the carriage with my sister and her husband-to-be, all feeling very sad and making our way to the Institute. As we passed on our way we came to a cottage where we were all known, and a shower of rice was thrown. Little did they know that the wedding had not taken place. When we arrived all the people were so happy and congratulating my sister. She and the bridegroom kept it a secret, but one or two noticed that the couple did not seem too happy. The problem was that arrangements had been made for them to leave England for Canada at the weekend so the only thing that they could do was to get a special licence and get married as soon as possible. This was done and they left for Canada.

My sister was in Canada for five years. Her husband had already been out there and had met the people he was to work for when he returned. It was a very large farm with cows and calves, and as soon as my sister and her husband arrived the owner just left them to do all the work and never fulfilled the wonderful promises he had made them. My sister often spoke of the hard times they had because of the severe winter weather and the fact that they were not paid any money. Life at home had been difficult at times but never as bad as this and she looked forward eagerly to a letter bringing news of home and was bitterly disappointed when none came. In the end they left and went into a town. The husband obtained work on The Transpacific Railway and stayed there until they returned to England.

THE GREAT WAR

As time went on there was a lot of talk of war. My father never stopped talking about it and stressing how we were all going to suffer in a way which was very unnerving for us all. We did not hear much outside news as there was no wireless and we only bought a weekly paper, but my father's forecasts about the coming war really frightened us. Although I was young, I always had faith in Britain and felt we should win the war if it ever started.

Alas, the war my father kept talking about did start and our lives began to change. I was at school when we were told a war had started and from that time onwards we saw many soldiers around the district and we felt safer whilst they were near. A camp was set up quite near us and there were concerts given by some artistes who came out from Hull. We received invitations to these and our family became friendly with some of the soldiers. As we went to school we got to know some very well and they would shout to us as we passed them.

Calling-up forms for the army were now arriving for all the men and there were very few young men around, although some who claimed they were doing important work were never called up. I remember my father getting his and making such a fuss about it at the time for he was above the age limit. All the younger men on the farm, however, had to join the army. I was sorry to see them leave and promised to write to them, which I did all through the war. My eldest brother, George, also joined up. Although he was only 18 years old and had not been called up, he saw his mates joining the army and felt he ought to do the same.

As the war continued, rationing started, and this meant that more forms arrived for all who were on the farm. It was my job to attend to these and it meant a lot of filling in forms and registering with the grocer for all the food which was in short supply. Coupons were needed for various types of food and these had to be sent with the grocery order every week. I was not attending school so regularly now as I had to stay at home quite often and help my mother, and I could cook almost anything by the time I left school.

We had quite a few soldiers sent to work on the farm as the fit men had left to join the army. These men who were sent to help out were not country men at all and not used to the work they were expected to do. We had a butcher, a bank clerk and a greengrocer and one who was almost blind, and I have to admit it was rather amusing to see how they all worked. My father lost his temper many time with them but there was no one else he could get and later the farmer's two daughters and myself had to help during harvest and other busy times.

We bought ourselves a land army outfit of breeches, shirt, coat, hat and the usual puttees for our legs, and had a photograph taken of ourselves. We looked quite smart for the job and were always praised for our work as we had been brought up to farm life

The author's eldest brother, George

and could use a fork or any other tool better than the soldiers. It was hard work as we always did so much housework even before we turned out to help outside.

Talk was mostly about the war and people were always saying that the Germans were going to bomb us, another forecast which came true. A warning was given in Hull by the blowing of a buzzer which we could hear and then we waited for the sound of the Zeppelin, which we also saw. It was very frightening when they started to drop bombs on Hull, one after another. So many were dropped that my father said they were 'shovelling them out'. When the Zeppelin returned it came very low over our house but I was so afraid I dare not look until I was certain it was passing over. We usually left the house during a raid and took shelter under a straw-covered shed. We had a pet lamb at the time which would keep bleating out and we were told to keep very quiet.

The pet lamb was one that had lost its mother and needed to be fed quite often. We kept it until it was fully grown and it went away with the big flock of sheep many miles away for some time. When it returned to the farm and was in a field with the flock, I just called its name, 'Nancy!', and it ran to me, followed me into the house, rubbed against me, and then ran back to the other sheep. I'm afraid we were not able to keep it and it was sold for £8. I should add, too, that during the war when meat was more scarce, we killed lambs at the farm and so broke the official regulations.

During the war the Government officials came to the farm to inspect all the horses as they needed them to pull the heavy guns that were used in France at that time. They only wanted the very best and chose some of our favourites. I shall always remember a horse called Star. It was brown and white with a white star on its face. This was chosen and also one called Smart and another called Rose. These were very fine horses and everyone hated the thought of their having to go away and most likely be killed, as this was something happening all the time.

As we were on the east coast we were now in a very important part of the country. One result was that there seemed more life for us all. Concerts and dances were held in the villages, I suppose the idea being to keep everyone as happy as possible even though there was a war on. This was the time when my elder brother, my sisters and I started going to dances. There was a dance class in Thorngumbald every Wednesday night and it was quite a treat to go, even though we did have to cycle three miles in the dark with very poor lights. However, that was the beginning of our dancing. I must add that we had to ask Father before we could go and this took quite an effort as he was not easy to approach.

When daylight saving started in the First World War we did not alter our clocks as the new official time would have meant men working in the fields in the early morning when everything was far too wet with dew. At the weekend when men went out we had to come into line with everyone else and put the clocks on. By now the war was at its worst and it seemed awful to be enjoying ourselves at dances and concerts while my eldest brother was fighting in France. We kept receiving field cards from him saying he was well and that there was a letter to follow. Eventually one arrived to say he had been gassed and was in hospital. After that he was given a short leave and came home. How glad we were to see him again – but he seemed so much smaller than when I had last seen him. Of course, I was the one who had grown. As a result of the gassing he had to wear blue glasses for a time; the damage to his lungs affected him the rest of his life.

He went back to France but it was not long after that we received a card to say he was missing. Everything now seemed terrible. We waited four months before we heard that

The author (left) and the farmer's daughters

he had been taken a prisoner and was now in Germany, and months passed before we heard from him. He was a prisoner for nine months and the war had finished by the time he returned to England.

We had to wait until after the war to find out what had happened to him because, while he was a prisoner, his letters were censored. He had been at Ypres and was wounded when the Germans shelled their village. The British moved on and he was left behind. He threw down his gun and walked down the village street, where he was met by a German officer and taken prisoner. The next thing which happened was that he was put into an old ruined cottage without windows where there were already other wounded prisoners. He had been wounded in his hand and mouth and was given a drink of beer. During the night the village was shelled by the British but fortunately the cottage was not hit. Next morning began the long journey by lorry to Germany. There were great big shell-holes in the roads and the lorry got fast in one and the prisoners were transferred to another. It seemed days before they reached the prisoner-of-war camp.

My brother was attended to by a Russian doctor whom he described as a 'cruel old beggar' who prodded with an instrument right through the hole in his hand. Paper bandages had been used on his head, and the wound wept through them. Food was very poor. They were given hard, dark bread and he brought a piece home at the end of the war to show us. There was also a lot of spinach and watery soup. Men who were fit enough were supposed to go out of the camp to work, but my brother never did.

We were obviously very glad when the war ended. We were expecting it to end and, when all the buzzers started to blow and the ships in the river began to sound their fog horns, we knew that it really had ended that day. The men on the farm were given a holiday and everybody was happy. I got on my bicycle and rode to Thorngumbald. Everybody was in high spirits and arranging a celebration of some sort. For a time there were dances and teas on everywhere, and, although rationing continued, we all felt it had been worthwhile.

But our happiness was short lived. The 1918 flu epidemic started and my people were down with it. One of my elder sisters, Ada, was now married and living at home with us as her husband, who was a soldier, was abroad. She was in bed with flu and I was the next to catch it; in fact, nearly all the men on the farm were ill. My sister died in 1919, and this was the greatest shock I had ever had, and life once again looked black. But one has to go on and this we did, although it made us wonder whatever would happen next.

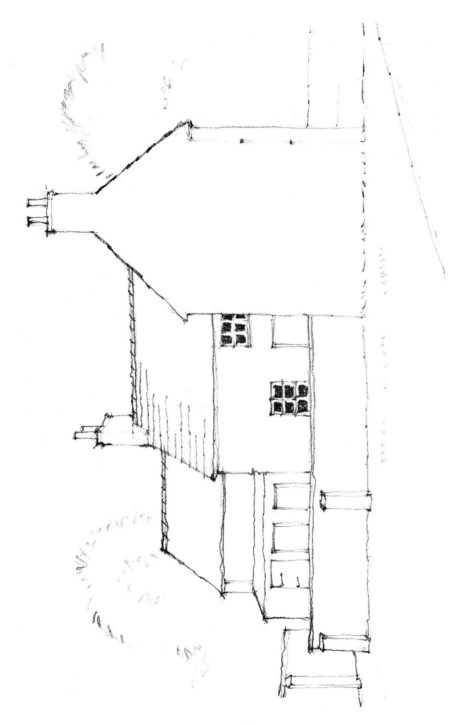

Another view of the farmer's house as it is today

THE BEGINNING OF THE END

After I left school I had the idea that I would like to be a nurse but one of my aunts was very discouraging and gave me a book to read and said, 'I don't think you will after you have read this.' As a result, I forgot all about my fancy for nursing. My mother was now finding the work too hard for her and needed some help as there were always four or five men to cook for as well as the family and it was suggested that I should stay at home and help. This meant, in fact, that I was responsible for all the cooking for the men in the house.

It began very early. My father always brought a wisp of straw into the house at night ready to light the fire next morning as we got few papers to use for this purpose. There was a large kettle to boil, the breakfast to prepare and a great pan of milk to boil for the men who had a pint mug each for breakfast, usually with cold beef, which they had at 6 o'clock.

One Shrove Tuesday when I was about 16 years old my mother and I decided that we would have pancakes; I was to make and cook them. In those days, as we had no gas or electricity, they had to be cooked on an open fire and this was not easy. The fire had to be nice and red without any smoke and I managed everything very nicely at first. I had just cooked one over the fire and put the frying pan containing hot fat on the hob. As I turned round, I caught the long handle, spilling the hot fat down my leg. Had any of us known First Aid, things would not have been so bad, but first one would say, 'Put this on it,' and then another, 'Do that,' until I think we did everything wrong we could possibly have done. I could not sleep for pain but tried to carry on working. I remember saying to a young man who was in the house that I thought my dancing days were over.

The doctor was called and, had this accident happened today, I would certainly have been sent to the hospital. Instead I had to be treated at home. My friend, the farmer's younger daughter, Kathleen, came in twice a day and dressed the wound on my leg. It was a very slow process and it took two weeks to heal and a new skin to grow. All this time I was in my bed and not allowed to put my leg to the floor. How I passed my time it is hard to say. I read quite a lot and everyone was very kind, bringing me books, fruit and other things. I did puzzles and tried to write poetry and draw. However, the day did come when I was allowed to get up and try my leg. For some time it hurt and I had to rest it as much as possible. It was always a very tender place and to this day I have an awful scar on my leg, though I am at least thankful that I did not lose the leg.

It was a great occasion when the elder daughter of the farmer, Monica, was getting married and everything had to be cleaned up in front of their house. I went to see her the night before she was married. She was in bed with a cold and her brother was so concerned in case she would not be well enough to go to church. However, the wedding did take place and she was driven to the Catholic Church at Hedon in a horse-drawn carriage. I had never seen so many people down on the farm before. There was plenty of food and drink for everyone and we all had a very nice time.

It was some time later that Kathleen, the younger daughter of the farmer, was married. It was rather a quiet wedding but very nice. She was the one who had always been a great friend of mine in her younger days and I felt sorry when she went to live away from the farm as it seemed our happy times together had ended and one realised what a grand time we had enjoyed when we were younger.

My eldest brother, George, had now left home and worked on the railway in Hull. He cycled into town each day for a time but the distance was too far and he decided to lodge in Hull during the week. When he came home at the weekend he always brought some little surprise for us and he was the one who first interested me in reading by bringing home magazines. The first he brought me was called 'Peg's Paper' and I always looked forward to it. It included a competition in which you had to guess the ages of film stars. I won a prize the first time I entered, a white silk blouse, and, of course, I was delighted.

Some time later my brother bought a motor cycle. This was a great improvement and later he taught me to ride. I was thrilled with the idea and it was not long before I was going for a ride to the villages on my own. What a difference it was just to ride along without any effort. I once took my cousin on the pillion for a ride but on the way I got my coat fastened in the belt of the motorbike. Luckily two young men came along to our assistance, and, although my coat was ruined, we were soon on our way again.

Later my brother got a more powerful motorbike which ran beautifully and I used to ride it too. One had always to be well wrapped up on these trips as you felt the cold somewhat. My mother bought my brother a flying helmet to protect his head. It was not a new one but it was very useful. I once got dressed up in it wearing helmet, coat and boots and had my photograph taken. Later I discovered the helmet had a name and number inside it but thought nothing of it at the time. Little did I know it was the name of the man, Alan Markham, I was going to marry some time later.

My two younger sisters had left school and were thinking about work. One, Amy, wanted to be a dress-maker as she was very clever at that kind of work. She went into Hull for a while but the distance was rather too much and she did not stay very long. The other sister, Norah, went to a farm as a domestic help and did not seem to be there very long before she was taken ill and had to come home and after a short illness she died.

Once again one wondered when all our sorrows would end and we would be able to smile again. Happenings such as these brought all the family closer together and my eldest sister, Annie, who was living in Canada was so upset that she wanted to come back home to England. A few months later she arrived with her husband and young son who had been born in Canada and we had a happy time meeting again after a number of years' absence. They settled on the same farm and lived in a small cottage which was always there for an extra man at the farm.

I shall always remember how happy and delighted my mother was when my eldest brother, George, who was entitled to a week's holiday, suggested taking her to visit her aunt who lived in Derbyshire, the one who each Christmas when we were small had sent us a wonderful parcel of gifts. At first my mother wondered if she could ever go, as at the time there were five men living in the house who had to be cooked for, and soon extra men would be employed as it was near harvest. I was delighted with the idea of her having a holiday and I knew I could manage the cooking, so all the arrangements were made and my father drove them both to the station. She started the best holiday she had ever had. How strange it was without her in the house!

She had five cousins in Derbyshire as well as her aunt and uncle and everyone made such a fuss of her as they had not seen her for years. They lived in a lodge at the entrance to a large hall with beautiful gardens; I cannot remember the name of the house – it was not Chatsworth, but very near there, quite possibly Haddon Hall. She returned from her holiday looking so well and happy and told us many times about her visit and the holiday she never thought she would be able to have.

Life on the farm went on very much the same year after year and one began to think how different it would be to live in a village or small town. Sometimes there was unrest in all the family and my father even began saying he was tired of work on the farm and that he would take any chance that came and leave. My mother was very concerned about this and began to wonder whatever was in store for us all.

Life went on, but at the back of our minds we knew that we should have to leave the old home in time. I began to feel that there were such a lot of things we were missing, as a visit to the pictures or theatre was almost out of the question. If we did go it was rarely more than once a year and always there was that long trail back. Now, we all seemed to be looking forward to the day when things would change for us all.

In the meantime I went out as much as possible – usually to a dance or concert – whenever I had the chance. I looked forward to going to Paull church each weekend and I joined a hockey club in Thorngumbald. We played each Saturday and visited different places. It was such a change for me and gave me an opportunity of meeting many people. This itself made me wish more and more that we would leave farm life. My brother, Eddie, who worked on the farm, was now going away quite often, seeking other friends, and it seemed that unrest was sweeping through the whole family.

But still nothing except the usual seasonal happenings took place for a year or two. My brother had his 21st birthday and I had mine some time later. My mother made me a lovely cake and I was allowed to invite a few of the friends I had made to come to tea. Once again one felt how pleasant it was to have some company.

As my birthday was in December, I knew we must have almost one more year at the farm before we would leave, as Martinmas which came in November was the time for changing jobs. Although things went on in the usual way my father had really made up his mind to leave farming and some time later he heard of a public house, the Borough Arms,[15] in Hedon, five miles away, which was coming up for sale. When he told us he was thinking of buying it, we all exclaimed, 'Never!', as we could not believe he would ever take such a step to that kind of business. However, he was delighted with the idea and talked all the time of how we would all be able to help him serving beer at the bar.

I must say that this was something I was very much opposed to and in those days I would never be seen going into a public house. Now it seemed that we were going to live in one! My mother was very much against it, too, although in the end we knew the time would come when the change was sure to take place. How we got through the last few months I shall never know: we seemed to have nothing else on our minds.

Easter came and I went to a dance with some of my friends from the village. It was then that I first met the man who is now my husband. I did not see him for some time after as he was away in the air force and went back from leave. We corresponded, our friendship grew, and he visited me at home. He lived in Hedon where the public house was and he could tell us all about it. This interested my father very much but it

---

15 Now renamed the Haven Arms.

The Borough Arms, to which the family moved in 1925

The author's parents on their Golden Wedding day

did not change my mother's mind. It was later that my future husband first introduced us to wireless. He brought a small set down to our home and we all thought it wonderful just to sit with earphones on and hear people in London. It was mostly the Savoy Band but it was wonderful to hear this in our own home. We could not get the earphones off my father – he was so taken up with it and kept saying, 'Can't you hear it as well?'

Eventually the public house did come up for sale and my father bought it. He had always kept a bank account at the Witham Branch of the Midland Bank in Hull but had not saved enough to buy the public house outright and he had to have a bank loan. A lot of people told him he was stupid to undertake such a thing and when he told the farmer that he was leaving there were some sharp words between them. 'Don't ask me for any money. I haven't got any!' the farmer told him. 'I'm not asking you for any!' my father replied. The 1920s were a bad time for farming, and the farmer never seemed to recover from my father's leaving him.

Now we knew that our time really was running out. It is funny how one starts to remember all the good times one has had and think that, well, it wasn't too bad after all. The leaving time seemed to come so quickly at the end. We began to pack our things, weeping as we did so. Everything had so many memories for us. The farm wagons came round quite early on the morning that we had to leave. There were no furniture vans in those days. Soon all our belongings were out of the house and my sister, Amy, and I were left to follow on our bicycles. It was the end of our life there. There had been bad times as well as good, but I would gladly live through it all again.

EPILOGUE

Now I have recalled my twenty-one years.
There have been laughter, sadness and tears,
But given the chance to live it again
I would go once more down memory's Bright Lane.

A M M

The Background to Back of Beyond

by

John Markham

Family Tree

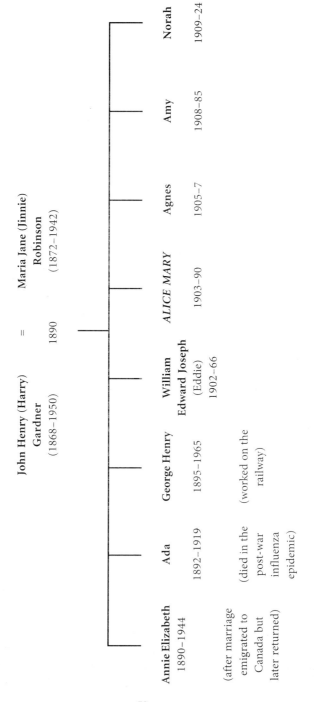

John Henry (Harry)
Gardner
(1868–1950)

= 1890

Maria Jane (Jinnie)
Robinson
(1872–1942)

Annie Elizabeth	Ada	George Henry	William Edward Joseph	ALICE MARY	Agnes	Amy	Norah
1890–1944	1892–1919	1895–1965	(Eddie) 1902–66	1903–90	1905–7	1908–85	1909–24

(after marriage
emigrated to
Canada but
later returned)

(died in the
post-war
influenza
epidemic)

(worked on the
railway)

LIFE AT THE FARM

Little Humber is a farm in the southern part of East Yorkshire known as Holderness, the triangular area which begins to the east of Hull, which is bounded on the south by the Humber, and reaches out to the North Sea at Spurn Point. Great fields (many now without hedges) stretch out to the broad, slowly flowing Humber, and blue-washed clouds float across the huge sky. The land is very flat, and many people have commented on the similarities between Holderness and the landscape of Holland. Others find it dreary and depressing. Sharp north-east winds can spoil the sunniest day, and the quietness and sense of isolation are sometimes oppressive.

In the early part of this century, before the advent of the motor car, living on a remote farm in one of the remotest parts of Holderness produced an intense feeling of isolation from the main stream of life. It was this strong sense of isolation in her childhood and youth – psychological as well as physical – which has made my mother value the importance of friendship and human relationships. The long lonely trek back along the dark lanes after the lights of Hull Fair and the companionship of the village hall have given her, I feel sure, a sense of being an outsider, an onlooker on a life she could not fully share, and her passionate interest in life and in people has developed from her early deprivation of these very things.

The fields on the farm were protected from the Humber by an embankment. It is a low-lying area which has suffered badly from flooding over the centuries. In the Middle Ages a number of villages with beautiful names, Tharlesthorpe, Frismarsh, Pensthorpe, Orwithfleet, East Somerte and Sunthorpe, were submerged by water and became the even more romantically sounding 'lost towns of the Humber'. One of these towns, Ravenser Odd, was a prosperous port on an island off the tip of Spurn Point and returned two MPs to Westminster. Edward I found the Humber area convenient for his anti-Scottish operations and granted it a charter. It disappeared from history about 1340 when a period of severe climatic changes occurred, the area was affected by storms and high seas, and the Humber washed the land many miles inland.

The farm, Little Humber, passed in Richard II's reign into the hands of the wealthy Cistercian monastery of Kirkstall near Leeds, which retained control of it until the Reformation when the monasteries were dissolved and their land confiscated. By the 19th century the farm was part of the estate of the Constable family, who were one of the most important land owners in Holderness, living in style at their mansion, Burton Constable Hall, and who in 1873 were reported as owning 10,981 East Yorkshire acres with a rental of £17,733.

There is no evidence that they took any great personal interest in this outlying property, though the annual visit of the agent was an event of some significance. It was also reputed that the Constables (an old Catholic family) preferred to give the tenancies of their farms to Catholics. I have no means of checking this popular belief but I suspect it is not far from the truth. It *is* a fact that the tenant of Little Humber who appears in these memoirs was a Catholic.[16]

The farm was in the parish of Paull and the church there, St Andrew's, was attended regularly by my mother's family. They did so very willingly and cheerfully (in spite of having to walk or cycle two miles each way, partly through an eerie and lonely tree-lined stretch of road which was known as Dark Lane and was said to be haunted) because it provided a welcome outing and a chance to meet people, and they made many friends in the little fishing village with its one 'main street', the cottages on one side backing on the river and subject to flooding when tides were high. Paull lighthouse at the end of the village street is (though long obsolete) still a well-known landmark for shipping in the Humber.

In the opposite direction was the village of Thorngumbald where my mother's grandparents lived and where she had a number of uncles, aunts and cousins. The children had to travel there every day to school, in the early days on foot, later in a donkey cart, and they knew all the families who lived in the village and their genealogical connections.

The nearest small town (though really only a village in size) was Hedon, five miles away. It was on the railway line between Hull and Withernsea, and the usual way of reaching Hull was to drive to Hedon, 'put up' the horse at the Shakespeare, one of the inns with which it had been abundantly provided in its days of greater affluence, and walk down to Hedon Station. Hedon was to play a significant part in the family story; when my mother's father decided to give up farming he bought (to his family's horror) a public house in Hedon, the Borough Arms (now renamed the Haven Arms).

Even for its time, therefore, it was a life apart, and relations and school friends from Thorngumbald who led a typical Edwardian rural existence seemed to have so many advantages: for them a visit to a shop, a church or a concert was not a major undertaking with the prospect of the inevitable anti-climactic ending of a long, lonely journey home along the dark country roads hanging over their heads and always detracting from the pleasure.

It is important not to romanticise a way of life merely because it belongs to the past and appears to be untroubled by the great problems which have afflicted the rest of the century. J B Priestley has emphasised the fact that 'during these years too many of the people could only be described as poverty stricken. A third of the population living at the centre of this huge Empire were below any humane level of subsistence'.

In spite of this, I cannot read these reminiscences without feeling that something has been lost, and that the life described had a quality which is missing from fashionable suburbia and commuter-land. Living was rough, tough, hard and sometimes crude, but at least it was a real, not a vicarious, life. Even the unpleasant experiences were real. A visit to a shop was an important social event which had to be planned – not some quick slipping into a supermarket on the way back from work. Boiling a kettle involved making a fire, which in turn meant gathering or chopping wood; baking and washing were activities demanding considerable effort and attention, and a skill which amounted to professional expertise. The weather and the seasons were all matters of great importance, and concern about them was not just a way of filling in a conversational lacuna. People

---

16 In 1948 R C J Chichester-Constable sold the property to the Crown. The present tenant (2010) is Mr Tony Leake.

spoke about 'the nights drawing in' with ominous undertones, because winter was far more than a minor inconvenience; it made everything much more difficult and placed physical obstacles in the way of social life. The rising in the blood felt by Chaucer's pilgrims in springtime was an experience understood by country people six centuries later.

There is nothing romantic about biking, drenched to the skin, against a head wind, or slugging your guts out with a scrubbing brush or a spade, but there is an enormous satisfaction and happiness to be derived from small personal achievements. Life on the farm was unremittingly hard and terribly limited by its isolation – a car or a telephone would have made all the difference. But an isolated life can have its compensations. It can be very rich and intense, and experiences make more impact and are memorable because they are not commonplace. There was a powerful network of relationships between the families in this rural area which has been largely superseded by the more affluent life-style of smart, but anonymous, housing estates. There was also terrible loneliness and frustration, but these are phenomena of every age and have merely re-appeared in more subtle but equally destructive ways.

The almost universality of motor car ownership has now transformed many South Holderness villages. In the post-war years there has been a great influx of newcomers who commute to offices, schools and factories from the desirable properties of the new estates which have been grafted on to the old communities. The original village still survives as a recognisable unit with its nucleus of church and Georgian and Victorian houses, and it gives character to what might otherwise be an impersonal and artificial conglomeration of houses. Newcomers, too, have often added vitality to village social life, which was far less thriving after the Second World War than it was in the Edwardian period, and some have attempted to re-create a way of life whose absence they regret.

The car has made these remote places so accessible that a journey there today makes one very conscious of the sense of isolation which must have daunted people who had to take hours over a laborious journey now covered effortlessly in a few minutes. Yet, although the invention of the internal combustion engine is rightly emphasised as revolutionary in its consequences, I am sure that it was the bicycle, not the motor car, which had the greatest and most immediate impact on the mobility of country people in the pre-1914 period. It is clear that social life improved both in variety and quantity for my mother and her brothers and sisters once they had bicycles.

A traffic census at Salt End on Hedon Road (now a busy roundabout near BP Chemical's industrial complex) on Saturday, 12 July 1913, recorded the predominance of the bicycle. Between 2.00 and 10.00 pm the numerator noted 1,012 cycles, and between 6.00 am and 2.00 pm 1,020 cycles. 'The humble cycle,' commented the *Hull Daily Mail*, 'is yet the most popular means of travel.' A regular weekly column in the same newspaper by 'Wheelman' catered for aficionados, and suggested interesting itineraries for the enthusiast. One recommended route for a day trip from Hull to Scarborough started rather comically by advising cyclists to begin the journey by taking the train to Bridlington – and so saving 31 miles of bicycling. His description of the journey itself was written in the 'literary' style affected by essayists of the period:

> We cyclists surely cannot be accused of being biased when we declare that there are no joys like those of the open roads. The reward of the labour we put in is a double draught of God's good air.

There is no doubt that this was the golden age of cycling, the time when riders saw the English countryside at its purest and best before the ravages of the later 20th century. By modern standards the roads remained remarkably quiet, and as late as October 1929 a newspaper correspondent, making his way in the evening from Hull to Hedon, was able to provide a poetic description of his tranquil journey:

> There were no other pedestrians on the broad footpath, and hardly any traffic on the roads; a few motor buses were on their way to Hull, and now and then a little motor car would slip quietly by in the opposite direction, and a jogging horse-drawn market cart or two, but otherwise the moon and I had the world to ourselves for most of the way.

POVERTY AND PENSIONS

Although my mother's grandparents seem an unremarkable old couple living in retirement, a significant event had happened at the end of their lives: they had survived into the Welfare State, and in January 1909 would have been among the first recipients of a nationally-provided old age pension. Many years later people still talked of going along to the Post Office to collect their 'Lloyd George' – or their 'Lord George', as they often referred to the beneficent philanthropist who had brought some measure of independence and self-respect into the lives of people who were unable to work any longer and would otherwise have been dependent on the charity of their families or the refuge of the workhouse, a fate almost worse than death itself. It was a dreaded building which haunted their lives and whose forbidding memory has still not been obliterated.

In the early 19th century the movement of labour had been from the south to the north, where the wake of the Industrial Revolution had resulted in greater prosperity and, at least as one compensation, higher wages: in the mid-19th century an agricultural labourer in the East Riding could earn 12/- [60p] a week, compared to 8/6d [42.5p] in Norfolk. My mother's grandparents had, as she shows, moved up to Yorkshire from Norfolk, a county depressed by poverty and one which a Norfolk local historian considers has been permanently weakened by the exodus of its more energetic inhabitants, not only to other parts of England but also through emigration.

The first pensions were of a very modest scale, 5/- [25p] to a single person, 7/6d [37.5p] to a couple, payable at the age of 70, but large enough to be attacked in the House of Lords by an impassioned (and wealthy) opponent of the Bill, the Earl of Wemyss, as a dangerous and evil social development:

> If, from sentimental motives, Parliament passes this Bill, I hold that you will establish a system of demoralisation amongst the working classes, that you will do away with thrift, that families will cease to regard it as an obligation to maintain those of their members whose working days are passed, and that self-reliance will be diminished.

Many old age pensioners simply could not believe that they now had an assured weekly income. In Bridlington pensioners began queuing one hour before the opening of the Post Office, and the Post Master gathered the impression that the old folks could not credit that the Act was really enforced and, 'fearful of being victims of the proverbial slip twixt the cup and the lip, were determined to be participants in the silver stream should it prove to be true'.

Fifty per cent of the pensioners were said to be illiterate, and the Post Office staff had to deal with a number of situations which occurred in the indeterminate area between tragedy and comedy. At Goole an old Irishman turned up, cap in hand, and asked innocently for his pension. 'Where is your book?' he was asked. 'Sure oi've no book,' he replied. When told he would receive one in due course he was said by a reporter to have left with a puzzled look. At Goole also 'two old veterans came together to identify each other. As neither of them could write it was found necessary to call a third person to witness the making of their marks.' In Driffield Mr James Carlin was reported as the 'first of His Majesty's Lieges' to receive an old age pension. He was more fortunate than an illiterate old stranger who, when asked where he lived, replied, 'Up yonder,' and pointed to the Workhouse. As a recipient of Poor Law charity he was ineligible for a pension:

> Softly and tenderly did this kind officer of the Crown break the news to him that he was debarred. But the stranger was a philosophic soul and he said to the Postmaster, 'Oh, all right. I thought that if I could have gotten this 'ere five shillings I could have come out of yonder.'

There was one nice piece of reporting of an incident in Hull. An old lady had been unable to produce any evidence of her age, but a reporter wryly noted that 'it was so obvious she came within the Act that the pension was allowed'.

Advertisers were apparently well aware of the new potential market opened up to them and one rather nasty advertisement stated:

> Old age pensioners – The first shilling should be spent in buying a bottle of Young's famous cough mixture – 'Sally come up!'

The air and shame of poverty and destitution overhung the lives of many: a realistic apprehension of what could happen at any time to anyone who had never had the opportunity to acquire the most modest capital to cushion himself against the instant effects of unemployment.

At Bridlington in January 1909 a soup kitchen in Quay Ward was patronised by hundreds of hungry people of a type one would not immediately associate with charity:

> None of the wan, starved looking neglected outcasts, waifs and children that one sees at the soup kitchen of a big city . . . The women, too, were warmly clad and had obviously only been driven to seek the charity of the soup kitchen through the prolonged tide of adversity that has of late almost overwhelmed so many of their bread winners.

The description of the soup certainly suggested that a very nourishing meal was provided for those in need: 550 pints of soup were boiled in the copper and the contents included fresh vegetables and copious quantities of meat:

> Shins of beef, sheep's heads, beast's heads, necks of mutton, pigs' cheeks and shanks of pork had all gone into the vast copper to produce it.

Not all the recipients possessed the appropriate dishes in which to collect their dole of soup:

> Now and again it was to be observed that the bedroom chamber services had been drawn upon to provide something to fetch it in.

ENTERTAINMENT

I do not think it mere nostalgic sentimentality to believe that the pleasure derived from the local dances and amateur performances surpassed almost everything now obtainable from professional entertainment available at home all day. Their infrequency made these occasions to be savoured both in anticipation and retrospect; every detail of every event was remembered and talked about for years until it passed into local mythology, and any references to the night when something or other happened triggered off knowing smiles.

People expected to be called upon to contribute and participate – there were too few around for many to be able to sit back in the role of passive spectators. It was a great time for amateur performances when audiences, uncorrupted by the sophisticated standards of the media, seem to have been genuinely grateful for the efforts of their neighbours and friends. Historians, however, must always be wary of viewing the people of two generations ago through a rosy haze. An announcement of a concert by the Hull Tramway Men's Band indicated that there were limits even then to an audience's indulgence and tolerance:

> This concert is to pay off the debt on the band instruments, and not as an exhibition of the prowess of the Tramway Band, as the majority of the people last year thought.

There is a refreshing naïveté about the reports of local social events, and their quantity and variety are in themselves impressive. At Easington in January 1909 there were to be performances on two consecutive nights of the cantata, *Alice in Wonderland* (surely a most ambitious undertaking for a remote village with a population of only 362). 'The Easington Concerts,' it was asserted, 'are famed throughout the neighbourhood.' At nearby Hollym, the local dramatic society were also to give an entertainment on two evenings, while at Withernsea, 'pupils of the School of Music established . . . by Miss Shaw in 1907 will give the opera, "Sherwood". It has been in preparation for months.' More cerebral entertainment was provided in the National School Room at Newbald in the form of a limelight lecture, entitled *A Trip through Basutoland*, by a speaker from Leeds. During the interval a large attendance was entertained by Miss Fryer, who gave an excellent rendering of *The Lost Chord* accompanied by Mrs Watkins, and Mr Golding contributed a recitation entitled *The Last Leap*.

This was the heyday of seaside resorts, and the nearest one for the people of South Holderness was Withernsea. A little further north was Hornsea, and, still more distant and more renowned, Bridlington and Scarborough. Each of the local resorts had a distinctive character and appealed to a different clientèle. One report analysed these subtle distinctions of style:

> Withernsea seems to possess a special fascination. There is something stern and wild about Withernsea and a spirit of freedom. Bridlington,

gay and giddy with its confetti carnivals, appeals to many Hull people for lazy holidays. Hornsea has a more quiet and subdued air.

Withernsea had been created in the wake of railway mania. If little fishing villages in the south of England could be transformed by the railway into popular resorts for the Victorian masses, then, asked local men of enthusiasm who dreamed of vast dividends on their investment: why should they not repeat this success in East Yorkshire?

Many shared the high ambitions of Anthony Bannister, a Hull businessman who was the principal promoter of the scheme. As one of East Yorkshire's most distinguished local historians, Kenneth A MacMahon, has written:

> The apparent potentialities of such a line to contemporaries were considerable. Not only was there the possibility of stimulating the growth of some coast village as a seaside resort, both for the benefit of industrial Hull and the East and West Ridings, but the financial advantages inherent in developing the wealthy agricultural area of Holderness were not to be overlooked.

Withernsea was not the automatic choice for the end of the line. Until the railway came in 1854 it was nothing more than a depressing coastal hamlet with a population of 109. However, it was its fate to be selected for the role of seaside resort, and a splendid hotel, the Queen's, was built by Cuthbert Brodrick, the architect who designed Leeds Town Hall, to house the visitors who would bring prosperity. Alas, to quote Ken MacMahon again:

> Anthony Bannister's dreams of a flourishing miniature Brighton on the Holderness coast were not then wholly achieved.

But, although Withernsea obviously disappointed the Victorian railway entrepreneurs who had visions of fame and fortune, and wealthy visitors failed to turn up in sufficient numbers at the Queen's Hotel, it is a seaside resort which has a secure place in many people's affections. For many, a day at Withernsea provided the most exciting and memorable social event of the year (as this account shows) and the apparently endless journey involved in getting there by horse-drawn vehicles increased the thrill of anticipation and tension.

At the beginning of the century there were excellent, well-patronised train services from Hull. On August Bank Holiday in 1911, 18 trains travelled to Withernsea and 20 to Hornsea, the earliest at 6.30 am. Communications have not improved: both lines were early casualties of Dr Beeching.

DRINK

My mother's attitude to drink as a girl was founded on her own experiences and observations and was not untypical of the time. She had probably never seen alcohol used as an enhancer of pleasant social occasions, but almost entirely as the one accessible way (apart from religion) of escaping loneliness and of assuaging intolerable circumstances. One, too, which ultimately brought great unhappiness to the lives of innocent people who did not drink themselves but who were connected in some way with those who sought this way out. The Irishmen who came over for the harvest each year worked hard all the week, lived in sub-standard conditions, walked to the nearest village or town to get blind drunk at weekends, and then engaged in the inevitable fights which formed the climax of their evening out. Similar experiences were repeated in many English working class homes.

'As is usual on Monday mornings,' reported the *Hull Daily Mail* in August 1911, 'the list of cases at the Hull Police Court today included more charges of being drunk than anything else.' The same edition included references to two farm labourers charged with being drunk at Patrington on the Sunday and to the claim of a brewer's traveller that he consumed 30 glasses of beer in a day. There was a charge, too, that drink was even a problem affecting those whose duty it was to uphold the law. In 1911, a year of serious industrial unrest in Hull, an 18-gallon cask had on one occasion been sent to the police station. 'It is quite certain,' one writer justly claimed, 'that by far the larger proportion of the work of the police is due to the consumption of intoxicants. Why has beer been supplied to the police during the strike? . . . They (the employers) set the seal of their approval upon the practice and have actually supplied the liquor.' This was, of course, the age of the classic comic postcards in which policemen were traditionally depicted with bright red cheeks and noses, an exaggeration which contained an element of truth. A letter from a working man to the *Hull Daily Mail* quoted Joseph Chamberlain's statement, 'Drink is the curse of the country', and drew attention to 'the most unprintable language' of the drunken girls on Hessle Road: 'Not infrequently have I seen girls taking running jumps onto a lad's back and I ask myself where are the parents and the police.' One evening at 10.45 pm the anonymous correspondent had seen a 10-year-old girl emerge from a public house with a full jug.

More tragic than the drinking of the Irishmen was that of the farmer's wife in these reminiscences, who must have endured unbearable loneliness in her substantial farmhouse in one of the remotest and bleakest parts of northern England.

RELIGION

Accurate, objective information about religious attitudes and habits is always difficult – probably impossible – to obtain. What is undeniable is that in the Edwardian period far more people attended Christian places of worship on a Sunday than they do today. The proportion of non-attenders in the population may have always been far greater than is popularly supposed, but the church, the chapel and religious influence played a major role in private, social and national life and affected those who never attended – even if in some cases it merely provided a standard against which they reacted and rebelled.

The church and chapel provided a focal point for social life and involved people in a network of relationships which went far beyond mere attendance at Sunday services. People who have taken up residence in local villages in recent years, particularly newcomers to the district who have no religious beliefs themselves, are often very aware of the absence of an organisation which can provide some element of social cohesion and integration. Clubs, associations and societies have to be created in a conscious attempt to fill this gap, which is aggravated by the declining status – even abolition – of the village school, as children are transferred to large comprehensive schools.

I am quite certain that the church sustained my grandmother through long years of isolation and despair. The long treks back and forwards on a Sunday were fully rewarded by the added dimension given to her life by the feeling she had of emotional and spiritual involvement in a fuller and more visionary community than could possibly be offered by the sometimes claustrophobic and introverted atmosphere of the two households at the farm. Her daughters followed her example. Their lives and language were formed and enriched by the repeated reading of the prose of the Authorised Version and Cranmer's Prayer Book. The Sea of Galilee, Bethlehem, Nazareth and the Road from Jerusalem to Jericho were, in their own way, as familiar as the Humber, the villages of South Holderness and the long, dark and lonely lane to Paull.

Figures of church attendance always show that in the Victorian and Edwardian periods, where religious influence was still all-pervading, those who absented themselves were in the majority. A *Daily News* census of 1902/3 revealed that in Central London there were 830,000 attenders, but 1.4 million non-attenders. In Outer London, where the suburban middle class was stronger, there were 420,000 attenders and 460,000 non-attenders. I have not seen any statistics on local church attendance later than those taken from the 1851 Religious Census, though in 1903 the Rev P Duncum, Minister of Spring Bank Presbyterian Church, Hull, claimed that, when one excluded all those who for some reason or other could not attend church, the reassuring result was that one-third of all those who could attend did on average do so.

The Victorian and Edwardian record of church and chapel building in Hull is statistically impressive. It was a town in which Nonconformity was particularly strong, and in which active Primitive Methodists and Wesleyans outnumbered the Anglicans.

In the second half of the nineteenth century 30 Wesleyan and 20 Primitive Methodist chapels were built in Hull, and in the early twentieth century three large central halls were put up. Directories show that every possible shade and permutation of belief was catered for.

There are very few East Yorkshire villages which do not have at least one architecturally undistinguished Nonconformist chapel dating from this period, and enmity between Church and Chapel was intense and survived until modern times. I am amused to see that my mother was rather ashamed of having attended a chapel service under the influence of her Nonconformist grandmother, and of her decision not to upset her own mother by telling her what she had done. The presence of an important land-owning Catholic family in the area, the Constables of Burton Constable, gave some degree of influential support to a minority religion. At a popular level there was still some evidence of ill-feeling between Catholics and Protestants, though the fact that the farmer and his family at Little Humber were Catholics does not appear to have caused any problems. Possibly, though, their attendance at Mass – along with the itinerant harvesters – was regarded as little more than an idiosyncrasy which had to be accepted, like other unusual aspects of life.

Religious worship was considered more applicable to females than males, and it is clear from my grandfather's attitude that, if the man went out and did the family drinking, the women were regarded by him as his representatives at the church to which he was – in his way – favourably disposed, but to which he also gave somewhat passive support. Charles Booth has a telling phrase about working-class boys who attend Sunday School under their voices crack, when they promptly claim 'their privileges of men and give up church going'.

SCHOOL

A new school has been built to replace the one attended by my mother, but the early one still stands. It is a typical Victorian Board School, plain and anonymous. In no way does it suggest the forbidding place of terror which it once was for many children.

Of course, the unfettered imagination of a child can transform trivial worries into nightmares, and children's impressions of teachers are notoriously subjective and their judgments selective and unfair. The formidable teachers of advanced years are sometimes reduced by retrospective knowledge into harassed middle-aged people, plagued by torments of insecurity about their work and positions. In this case, however, I have no doubt that the schoolmaster was as unpleasant as he is depicted as being; information which has emerged quite voluntarily from other sources has confirmed the picture of a cruel man of erratic temper.

Discipline both at home and in the school is far easier than it was in the early twentieth century, but Paul Thompson, in his book, *The Edwardians*, made the point that in the early years of this century it was at school that many children encountered for the first time a harshness and cruelty which they had never experienced at home. This is not entirely true in the account which follows; there had been examples of unkindness and unpleasantness at home but it must have been a painful experience to go from an isolated home and find in one's first real contact with strangers that they could be even nastier.

What is particularly sad is the way people were conditioned to accept intolerable conditions as an inevitable aspect of life. Today an active parent-teacher association and a leakage to the media would quickly remove the problems with which a generation of Edwardian children were plagued.

It was a deferential society, and one's whole upbringing and religious and cultural heritage emphasised the need to accept stoically one's place in life and to respect and obey one's betters. There were only a few brave ones who rebelled. This stoical attitude to life does help to explain why people can still look back, not in anger, but with nostalgic affection at times which were far from perfect. The feeling of being one of a crowd, all grinning and bearing it, engendered a warmth and companionship which, in retrospect, appear stronger and more important than the hardships suffered.

Camerton-cum-Ryhill[17] Board School, which served the village of Thorngumbald, was founded in 1875, one of a spate of schools built in that decade under the powers granted by Forster's Education Act of 1870 which had taken a significant step in providing elementary education on a national scale: where adequate facilities were not already provided by such voluntary bodies as churches, school boards were to be elected with power to establish rate-aided non-denominational schools. Revenue came from three

---

17 Described then officially as Camerton-cum-Ryhill School. Ryhill is now normally given the spelling 'Ryehill'.

main sources: the children's school pence (not abolished until 1891), a government grant, and a local rate levied by the Board, which in turn was elected by the ratepayers. The village school was, therefore, very much a local institution with a considerable degree of autonomy. In 1902 Balfour's Education Act abolished school boards and placed their schools under the control of the local education authority, in this case the East Riding County Council. The Boardroom of the school was converted into a girls' cloakroom in 1904 but it was still referred to by its original name.

The minutes and accounts of the Thorngumbald school from 1875 to 1903 survive in the Treasure House in Beverley, and from 1903 matters relating to the school appear in the minutes of the East Riding County Council. One major source of history which I have not so far located is the school log book for the Edwardian period. All head teachers were required to keep such a record of school activities and, although it inevitably suffers from being written by the head teacher himself – hardly an objective observer! – it often contains invaluable information about the school and the community it served. Professionally-kept minutes are usually too concise to be informative, and the controversial discussions and heated arguments which must have taken place are not reflected in the Board's bleak records of decisions taken and matters noted.

When I looked through the East Riding County Council Education Committee's minutes for the period 1903-17 I was very conscious of the dichotomy between the subjective and personal account of these memoirs and the official picture of quiet normality in the printed records. In October 1903 it was reported that the Head Master's salary had been increased (a previous application had been deferred) from £117 11s 0d [£117.55] to £120. In 1905 an application for an increase was refused, but eventually in 1905, after further delay, he received an increase of £5. Miss Emily S Duffill, referred to with some affection in this account, was appointed as a certificated teacher in 1905 at a salary of £60. I was interested to note that in 1905 my mother's grandfather was appointed a cleaner at an annual salary of £2 12s 0d [£2.60], especially as it substantiated the belief that in his old age he must have supported himself by doing odd jobs until he received his pension in 1909.

There were various innocuous entries about decorating the school and the Head Master's house, repairing the yard with sea gravel, and a major programme of alterations in 1908. The County Council official who visited the school reported: 'It appears the main room is over-crowded and should be enlarged. It could easily be lengthened if a piece of land could be acquired from the grass field on the east side of the school . . . The closets are on the privy system and should be converted to the pan system.' The whole enterprise cost a total of £695, and while it was under way the Church Institute was used as temporary premises.

Elementary schools of the period were plagued with bouts of illness, presumably aggravated by inadequate or unbalanced diets and ignorance of hygiene. An influenza epidemic caused the school to be closed from 4–23 February 1907; previous to the closure only 20 per cent of the 93 children on the books were attending. There were later epidemics of mumps, measles, whooping cough and diphtheria and in 1913 the school was disinfected after one of these closures. On two occasions illness caused supply teachers to be employed to replace the Head Master (no doubt to everyone's joy and relief). Would it be too charitable to suppose that ill health contributed to his irritability and bad temper?

One important curb on the independence of the School Board was the need to submit to an annual visit from one of Her (later His) Majesty's Inspectors, who would decide if the school facilities conformed to official requirements and, even more important, if the teaching and the attainment of pupils were of a sufficiently high standard to justify the payment of a grant from national funds. Once the school came under the jurisdiction of the County Council there were visits, too, from local inspectors. After hearing the grim accounts of life at school by people who still have vivid and painful memories of the period when they were reluctant pupils there a century ago, it came as a shock to read among the archival records in Beverley the euphoric – almost ecstatic – reports of local inspectors and HMIs on the school and the Head Master.

For example: 'This is one of the best schools I have seen up to the present. The Head Master is a competent man and has solved the problem of teaching practically the whole school without assistance. All the children are kept busy and quietly working, the Head Master giving his attention where it was most necessary. The discipline of the school was excellent and the tone very pleasing'; or, 'This is a very good school as previous reports indicate. The master is an excellent man. His influence I should imagine pervades the school and the children show every sign of being thoroughly well looked after.'

I cannot deny that there is a conflict of evidence here but it is not one which I think irreconcilable. History, after all, is largely an attempt to put into perspective and make some sense of a confused miasma of impressions, anecdotes and accounts, and to bring into focus the picture which emerges. In this case I cannot help being sceptical about the Inspectors' glowing praise. Inpectors are, as any teacher knows, notoriously gullible and easy to fool, and children very ready to co-operate in the charade of model lessons put on for their benefit. The reports refer to visits to the school paid by them on eight occasions in twenty-odd years and it is not so difficult to have everything conducted with perfection on a rare special occasion, particularly where advance notice has been given. There are many well-authenticated accounts of schools where children were rehearsed for the HMI's inspection in the early part of the century.

One sentence I read in one report on the school may carry more significance than its author realised: 'One of the schools that can safely be let alone.' Probably, too, there are hidden depths of meaning in the concise comment that the Master 'is a man of stronger and at the same time more refined character than many of our head masters. I should not say that he overworks himself but he certainly gives the children a thoroughly sound course of instruction . . . his attitude towards handwork is sensible, ie it is more or less the same as mine.' A later report notes that the Head Master is 'still going strong'.

Attitudes towards discipline have changed in an often revolutionary way, and it is hardly surprising if Edwardian inspectors found much to praise in a school where the Head Master did enforce discipline, obedience and concentration on work, all of which were regarded as supreme virtues, particularly for children from working-class homes. Praise was given in the reports to the Head Master's influence in ensuring a good attendance; on the day of one inspection only three children were missing although it was a wet day and some had two (in fact, three) miles to travel to school. I doubt if they dared stay away on such an important occasion, whatever the weather.

One cryptic item in the School Board minutes strikes me as throwing a revealing light on the realities of life at school. The father of an absent pupil, no doubt to stave off threatened legal action, made a formal written apology to the Head Master for entering 'in the Absentee List of the School Board a statement imputing misconduct'. I am highly prejudiced in favour of the recalcitrant parent.

In the Head Master's defence I have to admit that it must have been frustrating for a man with academic aspirations and ambitions to spend the greater part of his life in a small village school teaching very young children from homes which often placed greater value on help in the house and on the farm than on education and where there was little encouragement to achieve more than the bare minimum of academic attainments. To grow old and ill in this atmosphere, knowing he would never achieve anything more, must have been a bitter experience, and the exasperation which found its outlet in impatience and harshness towards the slow and unresponsive is understandable, though not forgivable.

The Master's beautifully handwritten timetable shows the stern and unrelenting programme which he set for himself and his pupils, but his explanation of religious education in the school, however sincere and noble in intentions, cannot be read without the intrusion of scepticism:

> There is no syllabus of religious instruction in use in the school. The children are taught Hymns – to say the Lord's Prayer – the Ten Commandments – the Beatitudes and four or five psalms. The Bible lesson is repeated orally after the master, who explains the same in as simple language as possible. Generally speaking the lesson has for its object the training of the children
>
> (1) as to their duty towards God
> (2) as to their duty towards one another
> (3) to become good citizens.

At least he managed to put the fear of God into some of the children.

It is also interesting to note that the official judgment on the two full-time female teachers of the school (though favourable) was never quite as enthusiastic as that on the Head Master: the very converse of the opinions of the children. 'The assistant mistresses,' wrote one Inspector, damning them with the faintest of praise,' are very fair teachers without being anything out of the common.' Another report did, however, sympathise with the way Miss Duffill's task in conducting an infants' class 'in three divisions' was 'made still harder by the fact that the children who lived by the Humber Bank more than three miles from the school often turned up about the age of seven knowing absolutely nothing.' My mother's account is written with feeling from the viewpoint of one of these children: it is interesting that this comment of a teacher who saw things from a different angle survives. There is much more vivid contrast between the reminiscences and that of an Inspector who wrote on his return to County Hall: 'Altogether I came away with a very pleasant impression of Ryhill School, its premises, teachers and scholars.'

My mother shows the highest regard for the Head Master's wife, a kind woman frequently upset by her husband's cruelty to his pupils. The practical lessons when the girls were taken to her house to learn cooking and housekeeping must have been a blessed interlude – probably one of the most progressive programmes of education at the school. For once the personal impression and the official judgment are in full accord. One Inspector noted in 1914 that he 'liked' the Head Master's wife and that he heard 'from competent authorities' that her teaching of sewing and home management was 'well done'.

The County Council's minutes show that the possibility of providing such lessons was not raised until 1910 when it was reported:

> This instruction in 'Homemaking', when carried out simply in the rural school, should prove of more real and lasting benefit to the girls than attendance at a Cookery Centre where the work is of necessity much more formal. In their own schools the girls can receive continuous teaching during the period of three or more years, thus allowing time for constant and very necessary recapitulation, such as can never, or rarely, be given in a Centre Course.

It was an innovation (which I know from personal experience had lasting benefits), one of the relatively few educational reforms whose results lived up to the aims and expectations of their original promoters. It is also amusing to note that when in recent years a local school teacher allowed girls into her home to carry out practical lessons the innovation was still sufficiently novel and newsworthy to receive press coverage.

Cynics may say that the basic aim of such instruction was to find replenishments for the army of domestic servants employed by all sections of society from the small shop-keeper upwards. There is an element of truth in this assertion but it is equally undeniable that many of the girls did learn something valuable about 'Homemaking' – first in their parents' homes and later in their own. It was an educational approach which suffered from many limitations but it did equip children to cope with the social and economic conditions in which they had to live and also earn their living.

Domestic service was at this time still the major outlet for female labour, in some areas probably the only outlet. 'Never again,' Marghanita Laski has written, 'would the pleasures of domesticity be sustained by the labours of so many people who themselves enjoyed few if any of them.' The peak period was the 1890s when 2 million servants were employed. Even in 1901, 1½ million out of 2 million employed women were domestic servants, all of whom must have experienced some of the problems associated with their type of employment: long hours, coal fires, lack of a hot water system, and the absence of modern equipment, cleaners and detergents, which meant that many jobs were laborious, time-consuming and soul-destroying.

The advertisement columns of the local press were filled with details of domestic vacancies. In January 1901, for example, one edition of the *Hull Daily Mail* contained 57 such notices, and The Ladies Registry in Pryme Street, Hull (the 'Ladies' were, of course, the prospective employers), dealt with domestic staff on a professional basis and announced its services in a manner similar to that of modern bureaux for secretaries:

> Wanted several good maids, good cook generals, house maids, housekeeper; also young girl for small family. Maids quickly suited.

The 'small ads' convey far more than they intended about the social history of England before the First World War and need no commentary:

> Wanted strong girl, sleep out, character required – 39 Hutt Street (Hull).
> Wanted respectable girl about 18 – two in family, 158 Coltman Street (Hull).

IRELAND

No hints of Ireland's political troubles and its struggles for independence were carried to the farm by the gangs of Irishmen who arrived each year just before harvest time. These itinerant workers were regarded by everybody, it seems clear, as inferior human beings, dirty and smelly, and prepared to exist on a sub-standard diet and live in an out-house in conditions unacceptable to the lowliest English farm labourers. Their only forms of cultural self-expression or assertion were to walk each Sunday to Mass at the nearest Catholic church, in Hedon, and engage in bouts of heavy drinking and ferocious fighting.

The men who came to help with the harvest at Little Humber were hardly a representative cross-section of their fellow countrymen but they were regarded by everyone in the district as typically Irish. It was an attitude shared by many, some in high political positions, a significant factor in the tragic history of Anglo-Irish relations over four centuries.

Father David Smith, the priest who ministered at the church attended by the harvesters, was a supporter of Home Rule, even if no indications of his political beliefs percolated to Little Humber. The *Hull and East Yorkshire Times* of 19 December 1903 reported him as being one of a group of Roman Catholic priests who provided moral support by their attendance at a meeting in Hull addressed by the famous Nationalist leader, Willie Redmond, MP for East Clare. It began with a patriotic song which 'set the pulses bounding with memories of stirring days long ago'. Father T R Murphy, the Chairman, said that the priest had been to the forefront in the struggle of the Irish people and that Ireland had been called 'the spoiled child of the Empire'. He pursued the metaphor with a vigour which still echoes in the newspaper report:

> They said, 'Spare the rod and spoil the child,' but it had been all rod with Ireland in a long record of misgovernment. The spoiled children were really the ascendancy class of Ireland.

In Holderness the only outward and visible sign of the influence and power of the priests was the fact that the local constabulary would call on their assistance as a last resort when gangs of drunken Irishmen got out of control. Stories are told of Father Smith being brought out by the police to wield his stick and disperse a melée of co-religionists outside the King's Head in Hedon.

It would be interesting to know how the local English Catholics (particularly the farmer and his family who would also be among the congregation) regarded these visitors who 'knew their place' and probably stood at the back of the church. (Parishioners paid rent for their individual pews.) One suspects that rigid class divisions were maintained and that religious solidarity was given no conspicuous practical expression.

THE GREAT WAR

The outbreak of the First World War was one of the few events in history which made a clear, decisive break between what went before and what followed. People who were alive at the time – and others who have only heard about it at second-hand – look back with growing nostalgia to the long Edwardian summers of the pre-war period before the sudden onslaught of the modern word in 1914. Distance often lends enchantment to the view, and unhappy memories have sometimes been absorbed and distorted by the Edwardian myth. But the impact of the War is not exaggerated in the minds of ordinary people.

It was a war which had been long on the horizon, yet when it happened came out of the blue and hit them hard. The newspapers of the period show this very dramatically. One moment they were reporting the usual holiday activities, visits to the seaside, bicycling jaunts and the annual Territorial camp. Then, with no period for mental readjustment, it was a grim and harassing story of enlistments and highly-charged scenes at the railway station as mothers, wives and sweethearts tried to catch a last glimpse of the departing men.

In my mother's story the War forms a natural break. After 1918 many aspects of country life remained substantially the same, but the War and its aftermath left a mark which could not be quickly obliterated and forgotten. Everything henceforth was dated by whether it happened before or after the War. J B Priestley, who has been influenced all his life by his Edwardian upbringing in Yorkshire, has written very perceptively of the sense of loss which was felt by people who knew England before the War: '. . . the Golden Age Myth of Edwardian England, together with its flood of nostalgic feeling, is not really based on garden party lovelies in big hats and tight skirts, nor on the low cost of living so that a poet might be housed and fed for a year on a legacy of £100, nor even – because it is important – on the fact that in those days there did not seem to be too many people everywhere. Edwardian England is a time and a land seen across a vast dark chasm of war. Over there the afternoons seem to linger in the mellow sunlight, the nights are immediately romantic. There is illusion here, of course, but it is not all a cheat: something *did* go, something *was* lost.'

The Zeppelin raids brought the first intimations of the horrors of twentieth-century warfare to English civilians, and there was intense indignation at this new and unsportsmanlike way of fighting wars. The Hunnish 'baby killers' were reviled by patriotic Englishmen for their devilish attacks on innocent unprotected women and children. Driffield was the first Yorkshire town to be raided, but in early 1915 Hull got a number of 'Buzzer Nights'. There were stringent blackout regulations and Hull became known as 'the darkest city in the kingdom'. The upper parts of street lamps were painted Oxford Blue and the lower parts Cambridge Blue; tail lights were required on horsedrawn vehicles and bicycles; people pushing handcarts, barrows and prams had to carry lamps;

the windows of the upper decks of trams were painted sepia white, the curtains of the lower decks were drawn and only two blue lamps turned on. Fines of 10s 6d [52.5p] upwards were imposed on offenders, and sums of £5 were common. General S O Nugent, who commanded the Humber Defences and issued all the lighting orders, even threatened to court martial those who disobeyed him.

The first Hull raid was on 6 June 1915. The buzzer sounded at 10.00 pm, transport services were stopped, lights were dimmed, and half an hour was allowed for traffic to leave the streets. There were no air-raid shelters and in the early days of Zeppelin raids the understandable tendency of terrified people in the centre was to try to rush to the outskirts. This was discouraged by the authorities, and refuge under the stairs was recommended as the safest place. There is a distinct air of naivety and amateurism about the aerial attacks, particularly in the inaccuracy of the navigation. On one occasion Goole, 23 miles away, was attacked in mistake for Hull, and a press item, supporting the prohibition of detailed publicity about districts which had been bombed, contained a germ of truth among its more fanciful speculations: 'One can imagine that the officers commanding the Zeppelin would look out eagerly for information in the English press. Every district named would be, as it were, a sailing direction for the next raid.'

Nor were the raids as anonymous as aerial attacks in the Second World War. On 6 June thousands in Hull saw the airship, the Luftseliffe 9, with its three gondolas, commanded by Captain Mathy, sailing over Hull 12,000 to 14,000 feet high, and looking 'not much larger than a cigar'. In the Hessle Road fish dock area one observer used an easily comprehensible simile: the Zeppelin was as large as a big steam trawler. People also noted the whirring of the engines and the clanging of bells in the engine room. In these circumstances the fear of my mother's family out on the Humberside farm that the noise of the animals might be heard by the Germans overhead is at least understandable. When a bomb dropped on a chapel in nearby Hedon an old man who lived a short distance away admitted that it was all his own fault for lighting a candle.

The Zeppelin passed over the river front as far as Marfleet, then turned and headed for the town, dropping two bombs harmlessly in King George V Dock. Then on the east side of the River Hull, where hundreds of acres of timber were stored, bombs damaged a sawmill and woodyard, although a well-known landmark, Rank's Flour Mill, escaped. The Old Town of Hull suffered badly, and in the 20-minute raid over the city 13 high explosive and 39 incendiary bombs were dropped, 19 were killed, five died from shock, and 40 were injured, all from the poorer classes.

The anger, outrage and desire for revenge needed targets on which to vent their fury. One of the nastiest episodes in Hull's history was the series of attacks on the shops of people with German names, including those who were naturalised British subjects of long residence and their descendants who were British by birth. A letter published in the *Hull Daily Mail* the day after the raid under the pseudonymous signature, 'Curiosity', posed a number of daft, ignorant and snide rhetorical questions: why was the least damage done to that of 'the life and property of the naturalised alien living in sublime contentment among us', was it possible they had a secret code of signals 'indicating where they may be fomenting their hate', or (rising to even more sublime heights of fanaticism and fantasy) was this immunity from attack their reward from 'the evil one' with whom they had been 'proved' to be 'in league'?

The appropriately named Elizabeth Tipler ('Carried Away By Her Feelings') was reported as being bound over for inciting a crowd to attack an alien who was being escorted to the Police Station; a young man, Arthur Jones, was charged with causing a crowd to assemble outside a tailor's shop where he attempted to fight the manager and his assistant; and a fine of 5s [25p] was imposed on Annie Bates for being drunk and disorderly and, in her inebriated state, trying to provoke a crowd to attack a pork butcher's shop, probably the business owned by Hohenrein's, a most respectable and patriotic British family, who, to avoid further problems, changed their name to Ross.

In war more than in peace time there is disturbing juxtaposition of emotions and events: the momentous and the trivial, nobility and nastiness. Newspapers contain examples of all phenomena. There are the heart-rending, ominous appeals of mothers asking for news of their sons who are fighting in France and from whom they have not heard for weeks, and there are the embittered, angry letters from the wives and daughters of men who have enlisted, pointing accusing fingers at others who should be in the army serving their country.

Both comedy and tragedy were in evidence at a camp gala held at Dalton near Beverley on 4 June 1915. It was the King's birthday and relatives had been invited to come and join in the sports at the camp where their men serving in the 12th Service Battalion of the East Yorkshire Regiment were stationed. It was almost like Derby day with crowds arriving on foot from nearby Kiplingcotes Station or travelling in a variety of 'traps, motor cycles, brakes and transport wagons', but the reporter was sensitive enough to detect that, in spite of all the games and laughter, 'frivolity was not always the dominant note'. His eyes wandered around the camp:

> There is an elderly woman talking quietly, happily and thoughtfully to an only son. Young wives with a child or two forget their anxieties in the reunion with their husbands. At the hedges by the entrance not a few men were expectantly on the look-out for a welcome visitor, whilst some of the jovial spirits teased them with a remark, 'There is no one coming to see you!'

If they could have foreseen the next three years there would have been a much greater sense of unease that day; so many were destined to become nothing more than a name on a war memorial.